The Nordic Banking Crises
Pitfalls in Financial Liberalization?

Burkhard Drees and Ceyla Pazarbaşıoğlu

INTERNATIONAL MONETARY FUND
Washington DC
April 1998

Cover design, charts, and composition:
Theodore F. Peters Jr., Julio R. Prego, and IMF Graphics Section

Library of Congress Cataloging-in-Publication Data

Drees, Burkhard.
    The Nordic banking crises: pitfalls in financial liberalization?
    Burkhard Drees and Ceyla Pazarbaşıoğlu.
      p.   cm.—(Occasional paper; 161)
    Includes bibliographical references.

    ISBN 1-55775-700-3

    1. Banks and banking—Deregulation—Norway. 2. Banks and banking—
Deregulation—Sweden. 3. Banks and banking—Deregulation—Finland.
I. Pazarbaşıoğlu, Ceyla. II. Title. III. Series: Occasional paper
(International Monetary Fund); no. 161.
HG3168.N63D74   1998

332.1'0948—dc21   98-14799
                                                         CIP

Price: US$18.00
(US$15.00 to full-time faculty members and
students at universities and colleges)

Please send orders to:
International Monetary Fund, Publication Services
700 19th Street, N.W., Washington, D.C. 20431, U.S.A.
Tel.: (202) 623-7430   Telefax: (202) 623-7201
E-mail: publications@imf.org
Internet: http://www.imf.org

recycled paper

Contents

The following symbols have been used throughout this paper:

. . . to indicate that data are not available;

n.a. to indicate not applicable;

— to indicate that the figure is zero or less than half the final digit shown, or that the item does not exist;

– between years or months (e.g., 1994–95 or January–June) to indicate the years or months covered, including the beginning and ending years or months;

/ between years (e.g., 1994/95) to indicate a crop or fiscal (financial) year.

"Billion" means a thousand million.

Minor discrepancies between constituent figures and totals are due to rounding.

The term "country," as used in this paper, does not in all cases refer to a territorial entity that is a state as understood by international law and practice; the term also covers some territorial entities that are not states, but for which statistical data are maintained and provided internationally on a separate and independent basis.

Preface

For many industrial countries, the 1980s were a period marked by economic deregulation, the removal of cross-border restrictions on capital flows, financial innovation, and increased competition in financial services. These changes were accompanied in most countries by a sharp credit boom, followed by a period of financial fragility, as lower asset quality and interest margins weakened banks' balance sheets. In a number of countries, the financial performance of banks deteriorated to the point where governments had to support some of the largest banks to preserve financial stability.

This study examines the banking crises in Finland, Norway, and Sweden, which took place in the early 1990s, and draws some policy conclusions from their experiences. One key conclusion is that factors in addition to business cycle effects explain the Nordic countries' financial problems. Although the timing of the deregulation in all three countries coincided with a strongly expansionary macroeconomic momentum, the main reasons for the banking crises were the delayed policy responses, the structural characteristics of the financial systems, and banks' inadequate internal risk-management controls.

The Nordic countries took very different approaches to bank restructuring. Although it is difficult to evaluate the outcome of these operations, several considerations seem to suggest that Sweden's approach has been the most successful. An important lesson is that the decision to adopt a comprehensive strategy enabled Sweden to weather a severe crisis, maintain the country's credit rating, and minimize the costs of the restructuring program.

The authors are indebted to Carlo Cottarelli and Liam Ebrill for their comments and support and to Francesco Caramazza and Steven Fries for their contributions to an earlier version of this project. The authors would also like to thank Eva Srejber and officials at the central banks of Finland, Norway, and Sweden for providing information and data. Comments from William E. Alexander, Manuel Guitián, Lars Jonung, Mats Josefsson, Arto Kovanen, Göran Lind, Peter Nyberg, and participants at the seminars in the IMF's European I and Monetary and Exchange Affairs Departments are gratefully acknowledged. The authors would also like to thank Sepideh Khazai and especially Kiran Sastry for excellent research assistance and Evelyn Almacen for secretarial support. Elisa Diehl edited the paper and J.R. Morrison coordinated its production; both are from the External Relations Department. The opinions expressed in the paper are those of the authors and do not necessarily reflect the views of the IMF or of its Executive Directors.

I   Introduction

The banking industries in several industrial countries, including the Nordic countries, underwent considerable change in the 1980s.[1] It was a period marked by economic deregulation, the removal of cross-border restrictions on capital flows, financial innovation, and increased competition in financial services. At the same time, distinctions between types of financial intermediaries became increasingly blurred. These changes were accompanied in most countries by a sharp credit boom followed by a period of financial fragility, as lower asset quality and interest margins weakened banks' balance sheets. In a number of industrial countries, banks' financial performance deteriorated to the point where governments had to support some of the largest banks to preserve financial stability.

The deterioration of bank balance sheets was particularly marked in the Nordic countries. With the collapse of asset prices and the onset of severe recessions that followed a period of significant domestic overheating, bank loan losses began to mount rapidly in the early 1990s. Given the thin capitalization of banks in these countries, such high loan losses greatly impaired the financial position of the banking system.[2] In Norway, where the crisis emerged first, banks' loan losses climbed from 0.7 percent of total loans in 1987 to 6 percent in 1991. Similarly, in Finland, loan losses rose from 0.5 percent in 1989 to 4.7 percent in 1992. The surge in loan losses was particularly abrupt in Sweden, where they jumped from 0.3 percent in 1989 to 7 percent in 1992. While losses on real estate loans represented a significant share of the overall problem, other sectors also experienced financial distress as the recessions deepened. In Norway, credit exposures to the primary, retail, and service sectors created problems, while in Sweden lending backed by commercial real estate proved problematic, and in Finland the large volume of loans denominated in foreign currency played a special role. Banks also sustained a significant amount of nonperforming loans to households—less so in Sweden—although write-offs have been relatively small in that market segment.

A banking crisis in the aftermath of financial liberalization does not necessarily imply that the crisis was caused by the deregulation. The Nordic financial crises, similar to experiences in other countries, were associated with unfavorable macroeconomic developments, such as economic downturns, declines in incomes, and depressed asset markets.

This study surveys the Nordic banking systems, examining competing hypotheses about the causes of the banking problems and providing some policy lessons. A key conclusion is that factors in addition to business cycle effects explain the financial problems that the Nordic countries have experienced. Although the timing of the deregulation in all three countries coincided with a strongly expansionary macroeconomic momentum, the main causes of the banking crises were the delayed policy responses, the structural characteristics of the financial systems, and—last but not least—banks' inadequate internal risk-management controls.

The Nordic experience demonstrates that if economic incentives are distorted by policy measures and the structure of the financial sector, then a negative shock may threaten the stability of the financial system. The absence of strengthened prudential banking supervision in areas such as real estate and foreign currency lending coupled with expectations of government intervention in the event of a crisis and a booming macroeconomic environment removed incentives for the market to impose discipline on weak banks. At the same time, these conditions prompted many Nordic

---

[1]See Davis (1995) and Llewellyn (1992) for a discussion of financial sector reforms and their consequences in Australia, Norway, Sweden, and the United Kingdom. See Cottarelli, Ferri, and Generale (1995) for the experience of Italy.

[2]Swedish banks had accumulated substantial loan loss reserves, which differentiated them from Norwegian and Finnish banks.

banks to increase their lending excessively, leading to a loss of efficiency in the allocation of capital. In all three countries, financial liberalization did not lead to an increase in savings as a result of financial deepening. Instead, borrowers responded to the lifting of credit rationing by incurring debt burdens that turned out to be clearly unsustainable. The resulting banking crises can be classified as "growth crises"—fueled by a rush for bank market share—characterized by a delayed response of market forces to weed out inefficient and weak institutions.

II   Banking Regulation and Its Impact on the Structure of the Financial System

In the early 1980s, the banking systems in Finland, Norway, and Sweden were heavily regulated. The regulations, which shaped the structure of their financial systems, were motivated largely by the same principles and objectives in the three countries. Besides securing the stability of the banking system, they were designed to maintain low and stable interest rates and—particularly in Norway and Sweden—to channel subsidized credit to specific priority sectors, such as housing and government. As a result, the Nordic countries in the late 1970s and early 1980s were characterized by widespread credit rationing. The chronic excess demand for credit fostered close and long-term relationships between borrowers and their banks and allowed banks to be highly selective in choosing relatively safer credit risks. At the same time, bank profitability was largely ensured by restrictions on competition from other domestic and foreign financial institutions.

In this section, we review the key banking regulations, in particular interest rate ceilings, quantitative lending regulations, and foreign exchange controls, that were in effect in the three Nordic countries prior to deregulation. We also discuss how these regulations may have affected the structure of the banking systems (Table 1).

Interest Rate Regulations

As justification for a policy of low interest rates, it was widely argued that investment in housing and long-term capital were particularly sensitive to the level of interest rates, while consumer loans (which received a low priority) were thought to be largely insensitive to interest rates. It was feared that higher interest rates would crowd out investments that were considered more socially desirable.

Lending rate regulations in the early 1980s were similar in the three countries. In Norway, such regulations had been briefly removed in the late 1970s, but in 1980 so-called interest rate declarations that set upper limits on average bank lending rates were introduced. Initially, these limits were meant to be changed by the central bank (Norges Bank) more or

less in step with money market and bond rates. In practice, however, lending rates were adjusted only infrequently.[3] Explicit limits on average lending rates were also imposed in Finland and Sweden. These limits were tied to the central bank base rate, which was changed infrequently, because such decisions were heavily politicized. In all three countries, particularly in Finland and Norway, lending rates lagged behind money market rates.

Because rates on individual loans were not directly regulated, banks retained—at least in principle—the ability to charge different rates on individual loans. Nevertheless, loan rates did not primarily reflect the perceived credit risk of the borrower, but instead depended largely on the closeness of the borrower's relationship with the bank. (See Commission on the Banking Crisis, 1992; Jonung, 1986; and Nyberg, 1994.) In effect, artificially low interest rates—reinforced by a generous tax treatment of interest payments that implied sharply negative after-tax real interest rates for household borrowers—exacerbated strong excess demand for credit.[4] As a result, a close banking relationship was in many cases essential for obtaining loans.[5]

Although explicit restrictions on deposit interest rates had already been lifted in Norway and Sweden by the late 1970s, deposit rates remained low and inflexible, apparently because of limited bank competition. Banks lacked incentives and opportunities to expand their lending and thus did not need to aggressively increase their funding through active liability management.

---

[3]See Cottarelli and Kourelis (1994) for an analysis of the relationship between financial structure and the stickiness of bank lending rates in a cross section of countries.

[4]Using a disequilibrium model of credit supply and demand, Pazarbaşioğlu (1997) finds evidence of excess demand for credit in Finland.

[5]When information is asymmetric, a close long-term banking relationship may also arise because it lowers loan costs. Banks' functions of gathering information and monitoring borrowers are in general discharged more efficiently as part of a long-term banking relationship with borrowers. See Stiglitz (1993).

Table 1. Banking Regulations and Their Impact on the Financial System

Regulations	Effects

Interest rate regulations
    Lending rates were controlled and were tied to
        money market and/or central bank base rate
        (changed infrequently).
	Limited price competition.

Deposit rates were linked to the base rate in Finland,
        but not in Norway and Sweden.
	Led to competitive advantage of banks vis-à-vis other
	        financial institutions in Finland, as only banks were
	        allowed to issue tax-exempt deposits.

Quantitative restrictions
    Reserve requirements
    Funding quotas from central bank
    Direct credit ceilings
    Liquidity ratios (bond investment obligations)
	Promoted extensive branch networks.
	
	Shifted portfolio composition of banks in favor of government
	        and housing bonds rather than loans to private sector.

Controls on capital flows	Prevented banks from resorting to foreign funding.
Prudential regulations No strict enforcement of capital adequacy requirements.	Banks held low equity capital.

No regulations on cross ownership between financial and
    nonfinancial institutions.
	Led to holdings of direct equity stakes in nonfinancial
	    companies by banks.

Other Foreign banks were not allowed to establish subsidiaries.	Prevented competition by foreign banks.

In contrast, Finnish deposit rates remained tightly controlled and closely linked to the central bank base rate until the early 1990s. Banks were allowed to issue household deposits with interest payments that were exempt from income tax, yet at the same time interest on deposits was tax exempt only on deposits that offered specific terms that were set by the authorities.[6] By requiring that all banks pay the same low interest rate on tax-exempt deposits, the tax rules encouraged banks to form a cartel-like arrangement, which severely reduced competition for private funds. The tax preference of deposit interest provided deposit banks with a competitive advantage by lowering their funding costs and may explain the relatively small role that other institutions, such as finance companies, played in the Finnish financial sector.

Lending rate regulations (together with deposit rate controls in Finland) meant that bank profitability was relatively stable in the Nordic countries because price competition—at least on the lending side—was ruled out. Moreover, low interest rate ceilings created "favorable selection" in the credit applicant pool by implicitly limiting the share of

risky borrowers. As a result of lending rate ceilings, bank lending was directed at the safest investments, and there was little need for banks to provide for credit losses and no immediate need to build strong management systems.

Quantitative Lending Restrictions

As restrictions on bank lending rates were eased during the early 1980s, the authorities resorted to controlling the volume of lending primarily through reserve requirements and liquidity ratios (i.e., bond investment obligations). In some instances, credit ceilings were also imposed. Restrictions on bank lending were supplemented with funding quotas from the central bank and controls on short-term capital flows, which prevented banks from resorting to foreign funding to finance their lending growth. Such quotas on lending prevented expansionary market-share strategies in practice, and, as a result, the close banking relationships were cemented further.

To restrict bank lending, the authorities imposed a supplementary reserve requirement on Norwegian banks mandating that lending in excess of bank-specific credit ceilings had to be deposited in non-interest-bearing accounts at Norges Bank. This require-

---

[6]Corporate deposits were not regulated.

ment, which was in effect from 1981 to 1983, was high enough to restrict bank lending.[7] Norwegian state-owned banks were subject to direct government control through so-called credit budgets, which, as part of the national budget, provided guidelines for the supply of credit.

Bond investment obligations, implemented as liquidity ratios, that required banks and other financial institutions to invest part of their assets in priority housing bonds and government bonds, were applied in Norway, but played a greater role in Sweden. By shifting the portfolio composition of banks in favor of government and housing bonds, these obligations limited loans to the private sector. Even though the yield on government bonds was often below market

levels, private banks—as well as life insurance and pension funds—were required to invest in such bonds. The Bank of Sweden also relied on moral suasion and on quantitative ceilings on loans to control the volume of credit.

In Finland, the central bank controlled the volume of bank loans by assigning each commercial bank a quota for central bank advances. Because banks relied heavily on the central bank for their marginal funding, the quotas had a noticeable effect on the volume of bank lending.[8] Similar quotas on central bank funding were in effect in Norway and Sweden.

Many borrowers were constrained in their ability to obtain credit from banks as well as other sources.

---

[7]The Bank of Finland imposed supplementary reserve requirements in the late 1980s, after financial deregulation, to curb the credit expansion.

[8]Deposits from the Bank of Finland at commercial banks were equivalent to about 10 percent of deposits from the public in the early 1980s.

Table 2. Structure and Market Share of the Banking Institutions

	Finland[1]				Norway[2]				Sweden[3]			
	1980	1985	1990	1995	1980	1985	1990	1995	1980	1985	1990	1995
Commercial banks												
Loan market share	49	49	61	70	26	30	30	30	37	38	32	32
Deposit market share	45	49	64	64	47	47	45	42	62	64	66	92
Number of institutions	13	7	10	7	24	29	22	20	14	14	12	13
Number of branches	880	959	1,037	729	565	702	602	488	1,479	1,424	1,345	2,239
Number of employees (in thousands)	15	18	27	20	14	18	17	15	20	24	25	39
Savings banks												
Loan market share	16	16	25	4	17	23	23	27	14	15	8	2
Deposit market share	23	21	18	5	45	45	44	46	32	29	25	8
Number of institutions	275	254	150	40	322	192	142	133	164	119	104	90
Number of branches	989	1,076	984	211	1,200	1,228	1,194	1,068	1,285	1,249	1,124	349
Number of employees (in thousands)	10	11	10	1	10	15	15	13	12	15	15	4
Cooperative banks												
Loan market share	23	22	14	27	—	—	—	—	3	3	1	—
Deposit market share	19	18	18	27	—	—	—	—	6	7	8	—
Number of institutions	372	370	359	300	—	—	—	—	12	12	12	—
Number of branches	822	852	800	667	—	—	—	—	380	389	373	—
Number of employees (in thousands)	8	9	9	9	—	—	—	—	3	3	4	—

Source: Organization for Economic Cooperation and Development, *Bank Profitability*, various issues.

[1]For Finland, loan and deposit market data cover commercial banks, savings banks, foreign banks, cooperative banks, and post office banks. Data for 1990 and 1995 include the post office banks classified under commercial banks. Data for 1995 also reflect the change in the composition of the savings banks, some of which were taken over by commercial and cooperative banks.

[2]For Norway, loan market data cover commercial banks, savings banks, postal system banks, state banks, and mortgage, finance, and insurance companies. Deposit market consists of commercial banks, savings banks, and postal system banks.

[3]For Sweden, loan market data cover commercial banks, savings banks, foreign banks, cooperative banks, postal system banks, mortgage institutions, credit institutions, finance companies, and insurance companies. Deposit market consists of commercial banks, savings banks, cooperative banks, and postal system banks. For commercial banks, 1995 data include cooperative banks, which were merged into a single commercial bank in 1992, and the largest savings bank, which became a commercial bank in 1993.

Even the amount of private bond issues and their terms—in particular their initial yields—were tightly controlled in all three countries. Specifically, in Norway, nonfinancial corporations were granted only small quotas for bond issues.

Borrowers also faced foreign exchange controls that were designed to insulate the domestic financial system and prevent international capital flows from undermining the effectiveness of domestic restrictions and regulations. The controls largely prohibited foreign short-term bank funding, although long-term borrowing by corporations was less restricted in the three Nordic countries. In contrast to Norway and Sweden, where foreign banks were not permitted to establish subsidiaries before 1984 and 1986, Finland allowed foreign banks to enter its financial system in 1982.

Impact of Regulations on Financial System Structure

Together with universal banking rules, the regulations led to the development of financial systems that were dominated by the banking sector and where money and credit markets remained insignificant. In 1980, three main types of deposit-taking institutions existed in the Nordic countries: commercial banks, savings banks, and, except in Norway, cooperative banks. These institutions together accounted for about 43 percent, 55 percent, and 86 percent of loans by the financial sector in Norway, Sweden, and Finland, respectively (Table 2). The post office banks, which also accept deposits, participated marginally in lending activities in Norway and Sweden, but constituted about 14 percent of lending in Finland.

In addition to these depository institutions, loans were originated by state banks (40 percent) and by mortgage finance and insurance companies (17 percent) in Norway.[9] In Sweden, mortgage and credit institutions and finance companies accounted for about 42 percent of lending, and insurance companies for about 12 percent.

The banking sectors were dominated by a few large commercial banks that offered a wide range of financial services and also played a considerable role in the nonfinancial sector because of the predominance of debt financing and the banks' direct equity stakes in nonfinancial companies. At the same time, the markets for banking services were de facto segmented: commercial banks focused on the corporate sector, while savings and cooperative banks concentrated on households and small businesses.

---

[9]The state banks are specialized banks financed through the budget to provide loans at preferential rates and other subsidies to favored sectors. See International Monetary Fund (1996) for more information on the market structure and evolution of the Norwegian financial system.

Table 3. Bank Profitability: International Comparisons, 1980–84
(In percent of balance sheet total; average)

	Net Interest Income (Intermediation margin)	Net Noninterest Income (Overall gross margin)	Net Banking Income	Total Operating Expenses	Pre-Tax Profit
Belgium	1.65	0.32	1.98	1.43	0.28
Denmark	3.13	1.09	5.33	2.80	1.48
Finland	**2.52**	**1.65**	**4.16**	**3.42**	**0.30**
France	2.50	0.46	2.96	2.01	0.37
Germany	2.25	0.51	0.57	1.69	0.63
Italy	2.91	1.09	4.00	2.57	0.62
Netherlands	2.17	0.71	2.88	1.84	0.39
Norway	**3.63**	**0.93**	**4.56**	**3.17**	**0.83**
Portugal	2.04	1.07	3.12	1.87	0.47
Spain	3.90	0.67	4.57	3.06	0.69
Sweden	**2.24**	**0.78**	**3.02**	**1.74**	**0.29**
Switzerland	1.25	1.08	2.33	1.33	0.62
United Kingdom	3.10	1.42	4.53	3.18	0.88
Mean	**2.56**	**0.99**	**3.55**	**2.32**	**0.60**

Source: Malkamäki and Vesala (1996).

As part of banks' liability management, deposits played a pivotal role as a funding source. Given that price competition was eliminated in Finland (where deposit rates were still regulated) and remained weak in Norway and Sweden despite liberalized deposit rates, banks competed for market share by building extensive branch networks.[10] Particularly in Finland and Norway, banking regulation appears to have supported cost structures that would not have been viable in a deregulated environment. International comparisons suggest that Swedish banks record the lowest costs (total operating expenses as a percentage of balance-sheet total) among European banks,

while Finnish and Norwegian banks have very high costs (Table 3). The ratio of Finnish and Swedish banks' net interest income to balance-sheet total has been among the lowest in Europe, reflecting relatively narrow financial intermediation margins.

In general, the sheltered banking environment, which was characterized by credit rationing and the absence of price competition, fostered a business mentality and banking strategies aimed at long-term relationships with clients. It also allowed decentralized credit decision making (often at the branch level) and lax credit risk management and encouraged cross-subsidization between various banking services. Profitability was largely ensured—although low in Finland and Sweden compared with other European banks (Table 3)—and most measures of bank profitability remained quite stable.

---

[10]There were no branching regulations for domestic banks.

III Deregulation

The regulation of the financial markets in the Nordic countries led to significant distortions in the allocation and pricing of credit. However, regulatory protection was not sufficient to isolate segments of the financial system from market forces completely. As one would have expected, market participants in the Nordic countries found ways to circumvent interest rate restrictions as the tensions in the financial systems increased markedly in the early 1980s.

Shortcomings of the Regulated System

Rising inflation—coupled with the reluctance to adjust nominal interest rate ceilings accordingly—made lending rate restrictions more and more binding and thus created ever greater incentives to bypass the regulated sections of the financial system. A parallel market (grey market) developed where lenders and borrowers interacted directly, and thus contributed to disintermediation (see Berg and others, 1993; Commission on the Banking Crisis, 1992; and Koskenkylä, 1994).

Financial institutions, however, were not bypassed entirely; they participated in the unregulated loan market through off-balance-sheet activities, such as guaranteeing and arranging grey market loans, and by channeling part of their lending through nondepository subsidiaries, such as finance companies, that were less regulated. The traditionally close banking relationships started to weaken when borrowers and lenders increasingly turned away from their "house banks" to find funding elsewhere.

It was generally recognized that the grey market did not unambiguously improve the allocation of capital because it created further distortions. By reducing the role of banks in gathering information and making risk assessments as well as in monitoring borrowers, credit flows were increasingly diverted to less information-intensive borrowers, in particular large corporations, to the detriment of bank-dependent borrowers.

Nor did the grey market enhance the quality of monetary policy control. To the contrary, the parallel credit market was seen as undermining the effective conduct of monetary policy, and, as money and capital markets developed, direct monetary policy instruments became less effective. The international trend toward indirect, market-based monetary policy instruments facilitated and accelerated the deregulation of the domestic financial system in the Nordic countries.

Reform Measures

In reaction to the increasing inefficiency of financial intermediation and the rapidly growing unregulated market, the authorities chose to relax most restrictions. In the process, regulators hoped to increase competition and efficiency in the banking industry in anticipation of the development of a European-wide financial market. To that end, bank lending and bank funding were deregulated to allow market forces to gain more influence, and foreign banks were permitted to establish subsidiaries.

The Norwegian Experience

During 1982–83, credit targets in Norway were exceeded owing to the increased circumvention of controls, and it became increasingly clear that credit policy had to be reformed to improve the efficiency of the credit market and the allocation of capital in the economy more generally.[11] Table 4 presents a chronology of selected reform measures.

As a first step toward liberalizing lending rates, the Norwegian authorities switched in 1980 to interest rate declarations that provided some flexibility in the structure of lending rates because they were ap-

---

[11]According to an estimate by the Norges Bank, the amount of grey market loans increased from 1 percent to 10 percent of the domestic credit supply to private sector and municipalities during 1978–83.

Table 4. Norway: Chronology of Selected Liberalization Measures

1980	The rates for individual loans were not regulated; rather the average level was regulated through interest rate declarations from the Ministry of Finance. Foreign borrowing by banks was liberalized. Under the new foreign exchange legislation, foreign currency exposure limits were established on banks; however, because the Norges Bank provided currency swaps, this measure imposed no constraint on banks' foreign borrowing.
1984	Supplementary reserve requirements were removed.
1985	Interest rate declarations were removed and interest rate monitoring was introduced. The bond investment requirement was phased out.
1986	Supplementary reserve requirements were reintroduced. The limits on the commercial and savings bank borrowing facility at the Norges Bank were increased markedly. Foreign banks were permitted to open subsidiaries.
1987	The supplementary reserve requirements were removed. Perpetual subordinate capital was excluded from the limitations on approved loan capital. The Banking, Insurance, and Securities Commission issued guidelines for assessing nonperforming loans and entering them in accounts.
1989–91	Remaining foreign exchange controls were removed.
1990	Foreign banks were allowed to operate through branch offices.

plied only to average rates.[12] But the effectiveness of these declarations was limited. Banks were partially able to get around the loan rate restrictions by manipulating their balance sheets, requiring borrowers to hold compensating balances, and charging extra fees for some services related to loans. Lending rates were further liberalized in September 1985.

Because they faced supplementary reserve requirements on their regular loans, Norwegian banks had a strong incentive to find other lending channels. In response, they expanded their finance company subsidiaries, which were initially not subject to reserve requirements. In reaction to the rapid expansion of the grey market, the authorities abandoned supplementary reserve requirements in January 1984, marking the end of lending controls in Norway.

With regard to bank funding, new rules concerning the foreign currency exposure of large Norwegian banks took effect in the late 1970s.[13] Under the

new regulations, a bank's foreign currency debt in the spot and forward markets could not exceed its foreign currency liabilities. However, as long as currency swaps were available, this restriction imposed no constraints on banks' foreign borrowing.

In a move to open the financial system to foreign competition, in early 1985 the government granted seven foreign banks permission to establish subsidiaries in Norway. All seven banks were headquartered in countries where Norwegian banks were also allowed to operate through subsidiaries. Foreign banks, however, were permitted neither to open branches in Norway nor to set up nonbank financial institutions.

The Swedish Experience

As government budget deficits widened and the public debt grew, the obligation on banks (through liquidity ratios) to buy government and housing bonds became increasingly distortionary—in effect, a growing share of deposits was transferred to the government in exchange for long-term bonds bearing low interest. As a result, the share of regular bank loans to businesses and households declined, and institutions that were not covered by regulations gained significance.[14] The considerable credit flows outside the regulated market challenged banks' traditional role. In response, banks attempted to bypass the interest rate regulations by establishing their own

---

[12]In July 1978, the government appointed an Interest Rate Commission to (1) propose fundamental guidelines for interest rate policy, (2) study how best to organize interest rate policy with a view to monetary and credit policy control, and, finally (3) assess how interest rate conditions affect income and wealth in Norway. The study concluded that deregulating the credit market would facilitate monetary management and reduce adverse effects of resource allocation. In January 1980, the Interest Rate Commission presented the results of its analysis, mainly advocating the liberalization of the credit controls and market determination of interest rates.

[13]These rules were introduced in 1978 on a trial basis and were made permanent in 1980.

[14]The grey credit market consisted for the most part of loans of nonbank financial intermediaries and trade credits.

Table 5. Sweden: Chronology of Selected Liberalization Measures

1978	Ceilings on bank deposit interest rates were abolished.[1]
1980	Ceilings on issuing rates for private sector bonds were lifted. Controls on lending rates for insurance companies were removed. A tax on bank issues of certificates of deposit was removed. Foreigners were allowed to hold Swedish shares.
1982	Ceilings on new bond issues by private companies were removed.
1983	Requirements on banks to hold government and housing bonds to meet liquidity quotas were abolished. Use of liquidity ratios to guide bank lending was discontinued and replaced by recommended growth rates for lending.
1985	Ceilings on bank loan rates were lifted.
1986	Placement ratios for banks and insurance companies were abolished. Foreign banks were allowed to establish subsidiaries in Sweden.
1986–88	Foreign exchange controls on stock transactions were relaxed.
1988–89	Swedish residents were allowed to buy foreign shares.
1989	Foreigners were allowed to buy interest-bearing assets denominated in Swedish kronor. Remaining foreign exchange controls were removed.
1988–91	Cash reserve requirements were introduced for finance companies in 1988 and abolished in 1991.
1990	Foreign banks were allowed to operate through branch offices and were entitled to participate in the Riksbank's clearing system on the same terms as Swedish banks.

[1]However, interbank agreements linking deposit rates to the discount rate continued for some years.

---

finance companies, which formed an important part of the informal credit market in Sweden.[15] The increased inefficiency of financial intermediation, the globalization of financial markets, and the perception that regulations were increasingly being circumvented led the authorities to initiate financial liberalization in the late 1970s—a process that continued during the 1980s.[16] Table 5 presents a chronology of selected reform measures.[17]

Credit and bond markets were deregulated first, followed by the removal of regulations on international transactions. The system of liquidity ratios for banks was abandoned in 1983, and in 1985 the ceilings on commercial bank lending and the restrictions on lending rates were lifted. By 1989, all remaining foreign

---

[15]Finance companies owned by banks account for approximately one-third of finance companies' aggregate balance sheet (Biljer, 1991). At the end of 1988, there were 290 finance companies with a total credit volume of about 10 percent of total credit.

[16]In the credit and currency exchange markets, long-established regulations caused a lack of competitiveness. The increased global financial integration and the rapid development of financial instruments made quantitative regulations inefficient (Dahleim, Lind, and Nedersjo, 1993).

[17]Various aspects of the regulatory framework and the liberalization process are described in Englund (1990); Gottfries, Persson, and Palmer (1989); Gottfries, Nilsson, and Ohlsson (1992); and Jonung (1986).

exchange restrictions had been abolished. In 1986, foreign banks were allowed to establish subsidiaries in Sweden, and in 1990 they were granted permission to operate branch offices.[18] But their share of the banking market remained small; by end-1994, the assets of foreign-owned banks represented only about 2.6 percent of the total assets of commercial banks.

The Finnish Experience

Under the traditional banking regulations in Finland, average lending rates were tightly controlled. Moreover, the lending rate ceilings were unresponsive to market forces and, in particular, could not adjust to banks' funding costs. However, as higher inflation exerted increasing upward pressure on lending rates, the Bank of Finland allowed a part of the banks' unregulated funding costs to be reflected in their lending rates starting in 1983. But, in 1986, the restrictions on average lending rates were abolished altogether, paving the way for market forces to dominate the financial system. Table 6 presents a chronology of selected reform measures.[19]

---

[18]The first foreign-owned bank branch opened in 1992.

[19]For a detailed account of the deregulation measures, see Abrams (1988).

Table 6. Finland: Chronology of Selected Liberalization Measures

1982	Foreign banks were permitted to open subsidiaries.
1984	Banks were allowed to lend abroad and to invest in foreign securities.
1986	The average bank lending rate was permitted to exceed by 1.75 percentage points the Bank of Finland base rate or by 50 basis points the average deposit rate on markka deposits.
	Later that year, regulations on average bank lending rates were abolished.
	Long-term foreign borrowing by manufacturing and shipping companies was exempted from exchange control regulations.
1987	The Bank of Finland began open market operations in bank CDs in the money market.
	HELIBOR money market rates were introduced.
	Credit guidelines were discontinued.
	Requirements on down payments on housing loans and consumer loans were eliminated.
	Restrictions on long-term foreign borrowing by corporations were lifted.
1988	Floating rates were allowed on all loans.
	Banks were permitted to use long-term market rates as loan reference rates.
1989	A supplementary reserve requirement linked to lending growth was introduced.
	Remaining regulations on foreign currency lonas were abolished, except for households.
1990	Prime rates were allowed as loan reference rates.
1991	Cross-border short-term capital movements were liberalized.
	Private households were allowed to raise foreign-currency-denominated loans.

Banks remained, however, constrained with respect to their lending rates in another (admittedly less restrictive) way. Finnish bank loans traditionally carried variable interest rates, and virtually all loan rates were tied to the base rate, which was set administratively by the Bank of Finland and tended to be relatively unresponsive to changes in market conditions. To enhance the influence of market forces, after 1985 the Bank of Finland allowed bank loans to be linked to other reference rates.[20]

Parallel to the liberalization of bank lending, banks' funding sources were expanded. For instance, the quota restrictions on advances from the central bank at the call money rate were lifted in 1984.[21] To give banks an incentive to trade directly with each other on the interbank money market, the Bank of Finland created a spread between its call money credit rate and its call money deposit rate in 1986. Finally, after reserve requirements on certificates of deposits (CDs) were removed in 1987, a domestic money market developed and gave the Bank of Finland the opportunity to conduct open market operations. As in other Nordic countries, the money market provided banks with new funding opportunities that permitted more aggressive lending policies.

In 1991, all foreign exchange controls were eliminated and even households were allowed to have access to foreign funds. Foreign-owned banks have been permitted to open subsidiaries in Finland since 1982.

[20]By the end of 1985, loans with a term of up to one year could be linked to the call money rate. Gradually, other reference rates were permitted, such that by January of 1988 short-term loans could be linked to the new money market rates (the Helsinki interbank offered rates (HELIBOR)), and long-term loans with maturities of more than five years could be tied to the newly intro-duced three- and five-year reference rates, which were based on the market yield on bonds issued or guaranteed by banks. The proportion of loans tied to the base rate decreased to less than 20 percent in 1996 compared with more than 90 percent in early 1988.

[21]However, in March 1987 quotas were temporarily reintroduced.

IV   Response to Deregulation

anks, just like other enterprises, develop their
business practices and behavior on the basis of
the prevailing regulatory environment, as the pre-
ceding section illustrated. Financial deregulation,
which was accomplished within a few years in the
Nordic countries, was a major shock to the system
and posed new challenges for borrowers and lenders
alike to adapt to the new environment. Indeed, the financial systems in the Nordic countries responded
quickly. As in other countries that underwent financial liberalization, the most striking development
was the significant rise in bank lending and risk taking (see Sundararajan and Baliño, 1991, and Bisat,
Johnston, and Sundararajan, 1992). This section an-
alyzes the incentives that led borrowers and lenders
to expand credit and banks to alter their loan portfolios and funding.

Borrowers' Response

Because the ability of some businesses and of
households to obtain credit had been constrained, a
substantial stock-adjustment response in private
credit was to be expected after liberalization (see
Hubbard, 1991; and Minsky, 1977). Demand for
credit was, however, also fueled by robust economic
growth at the time of liberalization. Bank lending
surged in all three countries. In Norway, the ratio of
bank loans to nominal GDP increased to 65 percent
in 1988 from 40 percent in 1984 (Figure 1). The
surge in lending in Finland and Sweden took place
somewhat later, reflecting in part differences in the
timing of financial liberalization and in macroeconomic conditions. In Finland, the ratio of bank loans
to nominal GDP increased to 98 percent in 1990
from 55 percent in 1984, while it increased in Sweden to 58 percent from 41 percent.[22] The effect of
pent-up credit demand pressure was visible in all
three countries, and liberalization resulted in a

credit-financed surge in capital formation and consumption (Figure 2) (see Lehmussaari, 1990). In all
three countries, the current account balance deteriorated and was largely negative following the liberalization (Figure 3).

Household Sector

The reaction of households to financial deregulation was similar in the three Nordic countries: households began to borrow aggressively and reduced
their savings sharply (Figure 4). Net household saving as a percentage of disposable income declined in
Norway from less than 5 percent in 1984 to –2.5 percent in 1985. The decline in the household saving ratios in the other two countries was more gradual: in
Finland, it fell from 5.7 percent to –1.6 percent between 1980 and 1988 and, in Sweden, from about
6.5 percent to –3.4 percent between 1980 and 1987.
Most of the household borrowing was channeled into
purchases of consumer durables and real estate. In
all three countries, household indebtedness (defined
as the ratio of household debt to net disposable income) reached record levels between 1989 and 1991.
In Finland, this ratio increased to about 90 percent in
1990 from 45 percent in 1980, and in Norway, to
175 percent in 1989 from about 90 percent in 1980.

In addition to an inevitable jump in credit owing to
the stock-adjustment effect in the wake of the abol-
ishment of credit controls, several other factors contributed to the incentives to borrow and the resulting
drop in household savings. First and foremost, in all
three countries, high marginal tax rates and full tax
deductibility of interest payments meant that real
after-tax interest rates were excessively low and
sometimes even negative (Figure 4). Because of the
generous tax deductibility of interest expenses for
both mortgages and consumer loans in an environment of relatively high inflation, households readily
exploited their freer access to credit after financial
liberalization. Higher asset and collateral values also
facilitated borrowing. The initial surge in credit contributed to a jump in asset prices, in particular real
estate prices. Expecting that the sharp asset price ap-
preciation would continue along the prevailing trend,

---

[22]The figures for Sweden do not include housing loans from
mortgage banks—most of which are subsidiaries of the major
banks. In Finland and Norway, housing loans were typically provided directly by the deposit banks.

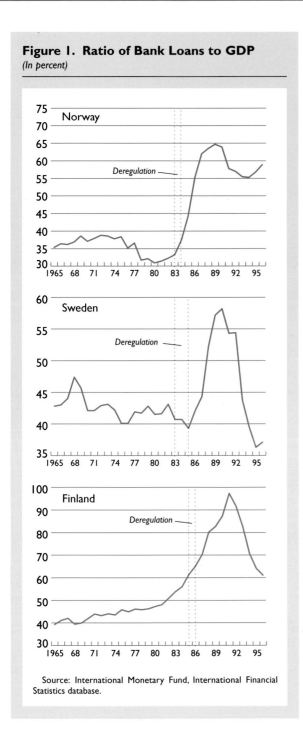

Figure 1. Ratio of Bank Loans to GDP
(In percent)

Source: International Monetary Fund, International Financial Statistics database.

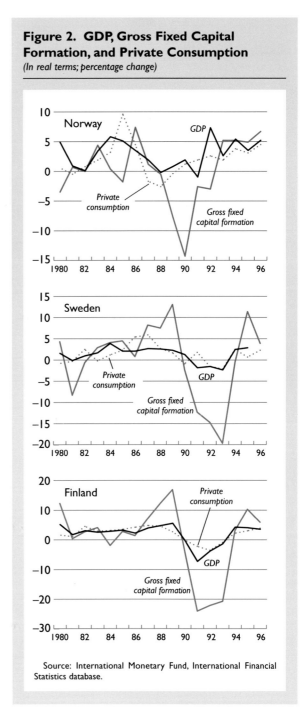

Figure 2. GDP, Gross Fixed Capital Formation, and Private Consumption
(In real terms; percentage change)

Source: International Monetary Fund, International Financial Statistics database.

many borrowers were willing to incur heavy debt burdens despite relatively high interest rates because they perceived considerable upside potential and limited downside risk. Moreover, low and declining unemployment combined with strong growth in disposable income (in particular in Finland where economic growth in the late 1980s was strongest among the three countries) fueled the propensity to borrow. In hindsight, it is clear that most borrowers did not anticipate the possibility of a surge in after-tax real interest rates on their variable-rate loans. Interest rate volatility picked up markedly in the early 1990s when monetary policy was tightened and the tax deductibility of interest payments was reduced.

Figure 3. Ratio of the Current Account Balance to GDP
(In percent)

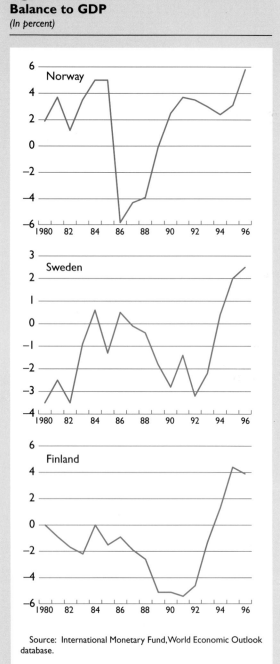

Source: International Monetary Fund, World Economic Outlook database.

Figure 4. Household Savings and Real After-Tax Lending Rates

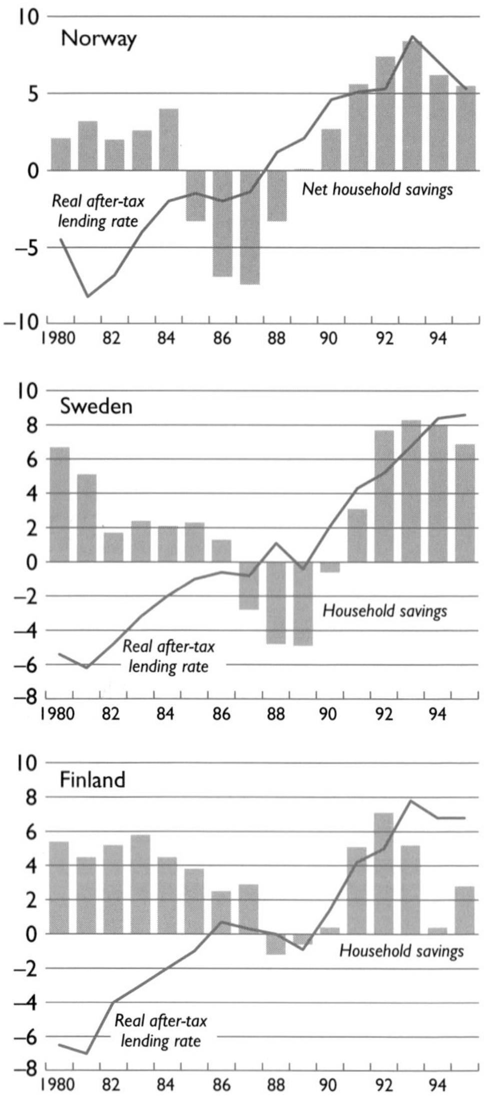

Sources: Organization for Economic Cooperation and Development Database; and national authorities.
Note: Household savings as a percentage of disposable household income.

Corporate Sector

The indebtedness of the corporate sectors in the three Nordic countries also grew rapidly after deregulation. Traditionally, corporations had been highly dependent on borrowing from financial institutions and, as in other countries with universal banking systems, relied heavily on debt financing. In 1980, the debt-equity ratios were about 3, 4, and 5.5, in Norway, Finland, and Sweden, respectively, compared with less than 0.2 in the United Kingdom and 0.25 in the United States (see Schuijer, 1992). A significant increase in private investment took place in the Nordic countries following deregulation, with the majority of activity occurring in residential and nonresidential construction, real estate, and services sectors.[23]

The lifting of foreign exchange restrictions opened up new opportunities for debtors to borrow from banks at what they perceived to be low interest rates in foreign currency. The surge in foreign currency borrowing was particularly strong in Finland, where in the late 1980s about half of the corporate borrowing was denominated in foreign currency (see Brunila and Takala, 1993). Given the large interest rate differentials vis-à-vis other European interest rates and the perception of a firm commitment to fixed exchange rates, a "convergence play" based on the belief that exchange rate parities were unlikely to change provided a strong incentive to borrow in foreign currencies even for corporate borrowers in the sheltered domestic sectors (see Goldstein and others, 1993).

Lenders' Response

Financial liberalization profoundly changed the competitive environment of financial institutions. In particular, the lifting of lending and deposit rate restrictions and credit ceilings opened the door to more competition. Whereas prior to deregulation obtaining a loan was often conditional on a close banking relationship and—as a result—a sizable segment of potential borrowers had difficulty obtaining credit, banks could use interest rates as strategic variables after the financial deregulation. The shift to more price competition weakened traditionally close banking relationships and impaired banks' ability to assess credit risks and monitor borrowers. It also facilitated the entry of banks and nonbank financial institutions into new segments of the credit market. Banks increased the role of fee income in order to lessen the dependence on interest income as traditional banking became less profitable (see Schuijer, 1992).

Heightened competitive pressures created considerable uncertainty about the new banking environment. In particular, the dense branch networks and sizable bank capacity that had been built up to compete for customers were becoming less viable. To secure their positions in the deregulated environment, many banks felt compelled to expand their lending aggressively by accommodating the surging loan demand, in particular to the real estate sector, which was thought to provide the best collateral. The higher risk taking was also supported by incentives that stemmed in part from banks' thin capitalization and

from moral hazard resulting from explicit or implicit full deposit insurance coverage and the expectation that no bank would be allowed to fail in a financial crisis.[24]

Changes in Market Shares of Different Financial Institutions

In Norway, during 1980–90 the share of state-owned banks in the loan market declined from about 40 percent to 18 percent. Reflecting, in particular, increased circumvention of regulations by private financial institutions, the market share of private banks rose from about 43 percent to 52 percent, and the share of private nonbank financial institutions almost doubled, from 17 percent to 30 percent. Similarly, in Sweden the credit market share of nonbank financial institutions increased from about 30 percent to 45 percent during 1985–90. The Swedish banking system as a whole experienced a decline in loan market share from 55 percent to about 40 percent (Table 2).

In Finland, savings banks as a group gained loan market share (16 percent in 1985 to about 25 percent in 1990) from other banking institutions (Table 2).[25] Because large corporations had well-established relationships with commercial banks and increasingly borrowed directly on financial markets, savings banks had to focus on more risky corporate borrowers, including small and medium-sized businesses that had previously been more or less neglected by the large commercial banks. Particularly rapid was the credit growth by Skopbank, the central institution of the savings banks, which increased its loans by 50 percent in 1987 and maintained high growth rates in 1988 and 1989.[26]

Changes in Loan Portfolios

Increasingly aggressive bank lending policies were accompanied by a noticeable increase in risk taking, as banks shifted their loan portfolios toward more cyclical sectors, such as real estate, construction, and services and toward loans denominated in foreign currency.

---

[23]In all three Nordic countries, the government promoted construction activity through various subsidies.

[24]In contrast with Finland and Norway, Sweden had no explicit deposit insurance scheme. In September 1992, the Swedish government announced that it would guarantee that all bank commitments be met on a timely basis and that no depositors, creditors, or other parties would suffer any losses (Sveriges Riksbank, 1992).

[25]See Koskenkylä and Vesala (1994), Koskenkylä (1994), and Solttila and Vihriälä (1994) for an analysis of balance-sheet growth.

[26]Skopbank was the first bank subsequently to encounter financial difficulties.

Most commercial banks in Finland (Skopbank in particular) had built up heavily concentrated loan exposures, mostly to connected nonfinancial corporations. Before1991, there were no regulations that limited exposure to individual borrowers. Although exposure limits were in effect in Sweden, some Swedish banks attempted to circumvent them by lending to property developers indirectly through finance companies (see Bank Support Authority, 1993).

After foreign exchange restrictions had been gradually lifted, lending to domestic firms in foreign currency increased in all three countries, but particularly rapidly in Finland. Finnish commercial banks increased the share of foreign currency loans from about 22 percent of their total loan portfolio in 1986 to almost 43 percent in 1991. Even savings banks, which in 1986 had almost no loans denominated in foreign currency on their balance sheets, by 1990 were lending 12 percent of their loans to the public in foreign currency.

Funding of Credit Expansion

At the same time as bank lending opportunities expanded, banks' capabilities to fund the rapid credit expansion improved significantly. Evidence from other countries suggests that, in the aftermath of financial liberalization, the volume of loans grows significantly faster than the volume of bank deposits (see Bisat, Johnston, and Sundararajan, 1992; and Cottarelli, Ferri, and Generale, 1995). The same phenomenon took place in the Nordic countries (Figure 5). Traditionally the Nordic banks financed their assets almost exclusively through bank deposits, whereas after financial liberalization some banks resorted increasingly to other funding sources, such as borrowing in the domestic and international interbank markets. In 1983, the Norwegian loan-to-deposit ratio was 0.9 for commercial banks and 0.8 for savings banks. By 1987, the loan-to-deposit ratios had risen to 1.5 and 1.2, respectively. Bank lending as a percentage of total assets expanded in Sweden by about 10 percentage points between 1985 and 1990, whereas the share of deposits shrank by about the same amount. In Finland, the ratio of bank loans to deposits, which had been rather stable in the past, rose from 1.3 in 1985 to 1.8 in 1990.

To finance their asset growth, some banks depended increasingly on the money market and on foreign funding, which tend to be much more volatile than retail deposits. The shift also meant higher funding costs. In Norway, for example, the interbank rate, which reflected borrowing costs in

Figure 5. Deposits and Loans
(In billions of national currency)

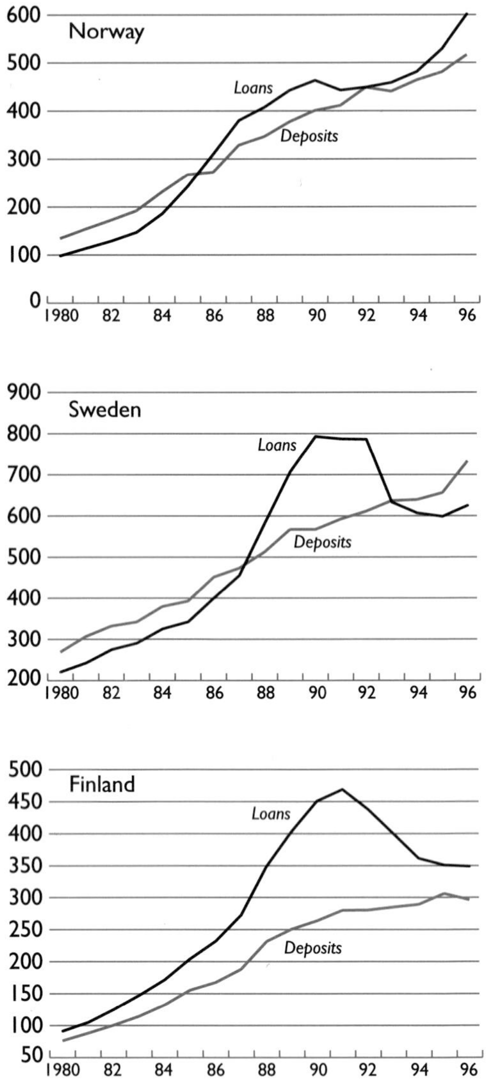

Sources: International Monetary Fund, International Financial Statistics database; and national authorities.

the money market, was more than 5 percentage points above the average deposit rate during most of the 1980s. Since bank deposits as a percentage of total assets declined and the share of money market funding increased, banks' funding costs rose sharply (see Commission on the Banking Crisis, 1992). In Norway, the lending boom was also partially fueled by liquidity support to the financial institutions by the central bank.

Figure 6. Lending Rates
(In percent)

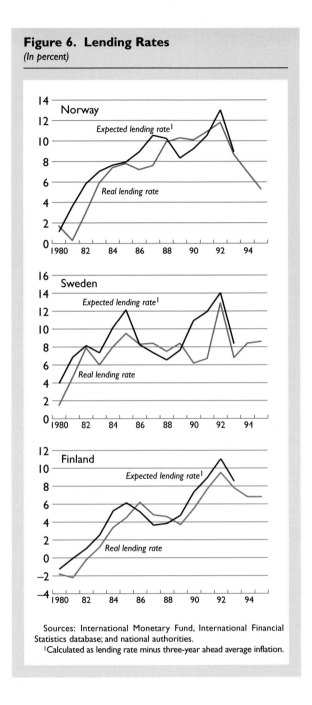

Sources: International Monetary Fund, International Financial Statistics database; and national authorities.

[1]Calculated as lending rate minus three-year ahead average inflation.

Pricing Policies

In theory, higher equilibrium real interest rates should be associated with more efficient investment, higher returns on capital, and higher savings and growth. However, very high real interest rates may also be associated with adverse selection and with the channeling of funds into riskier projects. They may also reflect a lack of credibility, country risk premiums, or banking system fragility (see Calvo, 1988; and Persson and Tabellini, 1990). Furthermore, following interest rate liberalization, the relative influence of domestic versus external factors in determining nominal interest rates depends on the degree of rigidity of lending rates and the openness of the capital account (see Cottarelli and Kourelis, 1994). If capital flows are unrestricted, the domestic interest rates will be largely determined by external factors through the uncovered interest parity relationship.

In all three Nordic countries, real lending rates rose before the liberalization of interest rates, reflecting the declining trend in inflation (Figure 6). After the abolition of lending rate restrictions, real lending rates declined to levels in line with international rates. However, it is puzzling that the rates on new lending remained below the money market rate until the late 1980s in Norway and below the yield on public issues in Finland. This suggests that banks did not raise lending rates to appropriate levels, which would have compensated them sufficiently for the risks associated with the rapid expansion of lending and for the increased cost of funding from money markets rather than deposits. What is more, the surge in interest rates coincided with a tightening of the tax treatment of interest payments and a decline in inflation that, as a result, raised after tax real lending rates substantially (Figure 4).

The net interest income—the intermediation margin—of Finnish and Norwegian banks declined during the liberalization period (1985–90) compared with the preliberalization period (1980–85) (Tables 7 and 8). This decline was particularly evident for Norwegian commercial banks and the Finnish savings banks. It can be explained by four main phenomena: increased competition between financial institutions, the growing dependence on more expensive money market funding rather than deposits, an increase in nonaccrual loans,[27] and the reduction in credit commissions. (See Berg and others, 1993; and Berg, Forsund, and Jansen, 1992).

The decline in the interest rate spreads at the time of the credit boom also suggests more intense competition among financial institutions.[28] The net interest income of cooperatives and savings banks increased in Sweden during the deregulation period reflecting the reallocation of bank portfolios from government bonds to private sector loans (Table 9) (see Dahleim, Goran, and Nedersjo, 1993; and Lind and Nerdersjo, 1994). In contrast, Finnish banks' in-

---

[27]Nonaccrual loans are potential bad loans that have not yet been entered as losses, but are instead debited to the banks' earnings.

[28]See Cottarelli, Ferri, and Generale (1995) on the experience of Italy and other European countries.

Table 7. Finland: Bank Profitability
(In percent of average total assets)

	1980	1981	1982	1983	1984	1985	1986	1987	1988	1989	1990	1991	1992	1993	1994	1995
Commercial banks																
Net interest income	2.28	2.19	2.14	1.68	1.64	1.65	1.24	1.53	1.59	1.36	1.51	1.25	1.12	1.37	1.36	1.44
Operating expenses	3.59	3.38	3.16	2.88	2.86	2.80	2.59	2.58	2.81	2.64	2.61	4.02	4.35	4.54	3.96	3.32
Loan loss provisions	0.02	0.03	0.06	0.07	0.07	0.08	0.11	0.17	0.23	0.27	0.30	0.96	2.30	2.42	1.00	—
Profits before taxes	0.71	0.97	0.99	0.70	0.80	1.09	0.82	0.90	1.09	0.46	0.38	−0.73	−1.93	−1.76	−1.12	−0.55
Cooperative banks																
Net interest margins	3.71	3.73	3.66	3.50	3.34	3.36	3.19	3.27	3.21	2.90	3.10	2.98	2.47	2.99	3.41	3.28
Operating expenses	4.52	4.49	4.66	4.50	4.49	4.03	4.08	4.14	4.03	3.83	3.84	4.35	5.12	6.28	6.19	5.03
Loan loss provisions	—	—	—	0.02	0.02	0.02	0.06	0.19	0.19	0.16	0.18	0.39	1.13	2.24	0.91	—
Profits before taxes	0.67	0.71	0.77	0.69	0.64	0.75	0.67	0.73	0.96	0.60	0.78	0.76	0.03	−1.65	−1.17	−0.02
Savings banks																
Net interest income	3.57	3.57	3.83	3.50	3.10	3.28	3.28	3.27	3.05	2.65	2.53	2.09	0.36	1.50	0.47	2.32
Operating expenses	4.23	4.20	4.26	4.11	4.09	4.48	4.61	4.72	4.43	3.94	3.54	4.76	12.38	6.93	3.78	2.61
Loan loss provisions	—	—	—	—	—	0.04	0.04	0.11	0.12	0.18	0.36	0.94	6.80	3.30	1.85	—
Profits before taxes	0.59	0.66	0.69	0.53	0.40	0.60	0.64	0.72	0.76	0.45	0.56	−0.41	−9.29	−4.94	−2.05	0.41

Sources: Organization for Economic Cooperation and Development, *Bank Profitability* (1996); and Bank of Finland.

termediation margins were among the lowest of European banks (Table 10).

Overall, the vulnerability of banks to credit losses increased in all three countries because no additional operating profits were being generated during the lending boom to compensate for the greater lending risks. Unlike most other European countries, the banking systems in the three Nordic countries all recorded below-average pre-tax profits during the postliberalization period (Table 10).

Incentives for Increased Risk Taking

A central question about the Nordic banking experience in the late 1980s is, what was the banks' economic motivation and their underlying incentives for

Table 8. Norway: Bank Profitability
(In percent of average total assets)

	1980	1981	1982	1983	1984	1985	1986	1987	1988	1989	1990	1991	1992	1993	1994	1995
Commercial banks																
Net interest income	3.17	3.06	3.03	3.39	3.10	2.77	2.78	2.71	2.62	2.98	2.55	2.45	2.78	3.07	2.78	2.76
Operating expenses	3.55	3.47	3.27	3.31	3.27	3.11	2.90	2.92	2.68	2.64	2.62	3.15	2.48	2.38	2.57	2.76
Loan loss provisions	0.13	0.07	0.17	0.20	0.24	0.35	0.50	1.03	1.57	1.60	1.96	4.28	2.25	1.41	0.10	0.01
Profits before taxes	0.85	0.99	0.81	1.18	1.17	0.92	0.95	−0.04	−0.13	0.04	−1.17	−4.29	−1.25	0.58	1.21	2.00
Savings banks																
Net interest income	3.92	4.52	4.60	4.64	4.44	3.87	3.70	4.03	3.62	4.14	3.85	3.79	4.34	4.73	4.14	3.91
Operating expenses	2.97	3.18	3.32	3.47	3.47	3.38	3.24	3.15	3.07	3.08	3.09	3.34	2.96	2.92	2.90	2.91
Loan loss provision	0.04	0.06	0.07	0.13	0.15	0.18	0.27	0.84	1.23	2.24	2.05	2.11	1.83	1.19	0.40	0.13
Profits before taxes	1.03	1.56	2.12	1.35	1.23	0.86	0.94	0.63	−0.04	−0.30	−0.77	−1.21	0.04	2.03	1.28	1.87

Sources: Organization for Economic Cooperation and Development, *Bank Profitability* (1996); and Norges Bank.

Table 9. Sweden: Bank Profitability
(In percent of average total assets)

	1980	1981	1982	1983	1984	1985	1986	1987	1988	1989	1990	1991	1992	1993	1994	1995
Commercial banks																
Net interest income	2.10	2.15	1.99	2.27	2.21	1.99	2.61	2.49	2.44	2.15	2.08	2.09	2.19	2.72	2.56	2.68
Operating expenses	2.00	2.05	2.16	1.94	2.06	1.89	2.19	1.93	1.90	1.58	2.21	3.38	5.35	6.46	3.25	2.98
Loan loss provisions	0.05	0.11	0.35	0.28	0.39	0.23	0.34	0.24	0.17	0.18	0.62	1.83	3.37	3.18	2.51	2.00
Profits before taxes	1.07	1.13	0.91	1.38	1.12	1.11	1.85	1.29	1.45	1.22	0.68	−0.50	−2.31	−1.22	0.98	1.33
Cooperative banks																
Net interest income	2.72	3.15	3.33	3.69	3.70	4.08	4.50	4.50	4.69	4.84	3.87	3.94	—	—	—	—
Operating expenses	2.15	2.15	2.17	2.27	2.53	2.80	2.77	3.10	3.04	2.96	2.16	2.17	—	—	—	—
Loan loss provision	0.01	0.02	0.05	0.07	0.07	0.18	0.18	0.19	0.18	0.31	0.65	2.80	—	—	—	—
Profits before taxes	0.56	0.98	1.12	1.35	1.10	1.10	1.56	1.21	1.47	1.57	1.06	−1.03	—	—	—	—
Savings banks																
Net interest income	2.64	3.09	3.22	3.60	3.59	3.94	4.21	4.05	4.13	4.11	4.55	4.53	4.17	6.83	4.90	4.95
Operating expenses	2.41	2.38	2.54	2.63	3.19	3.70	4.00	4.02	3.95	3.92	4.39	7.23	9.33	6.12	4.42	4.61
Loan loss provision	0.02	0.03	0.07	0.11	0.16	0.29	0.42	0.28	0.29	0.36	1.09	3.85	4.46	2.15	2.01	2.00
Profits before taxes	0.75	1.19	1.20	1.39	1.18	1.26	1.60	1.14	1.34	1.21	1.04	−1.79	−2.82	1.54	1.74	1.58

Sources: Organization for Economic Cooperation and Development, *Bank Profitability* (1996); and Sveriges Riksbank.

the sharp increase in bank lending, and more important, in risk taking? Several factors appear to have contributed to the banks' behavior. These include moral hazard incentives stemming from implicit state policies that no bank will fail; reduced bank franchise values owing to lower economic rents and cost rigidities in the banking industry after liberalization; and insufficient adjustment of internal control incentives and business practices to the new environment (see Guttentag and Herring, 1986).

Table 10. Bank Profitability: International Comparisons, 1985–89
(In percent of balance sheet total; average)

	Net Interest Income (Intermediation margin)	Net Noninterest Income (Overall gross margin)	Net Banking Income	Total Operating Expenses	Pre-Tax Profit
Belgium	1.61	0.44	2.05	1.37	0.31
Denmark	2.49	1.09	3.58	2.05	0.81
Finland	**1.94**	**1.81**	**3.75**	**2.85**	**0.37**
France	2.25	0.41	2.66	1.80	0.32
Germany	2.13	0.57	2.69	1.73	0.59
Italy	3.06	1.18	4.24	2.73	0.94
Netherlands	2.16	0.78	2.94	1.94	0.67
Norway	**3.16**	**1.07**	**4.23**	**2.90**	**0.23**
Portugal	3.01	0.69	3.70	2.08	0.55
Spain	3.87	0.81	4.67	2.98	1.02
Sweden	**2.68**	**1.04**	**3.73**	**2.06**	**0.56**
Switzerland	1.32	1.29	2.61	1.44	0.68
United Kingdom	3.03	1.74	4.76	3.10	0.81
Mean	**2.52**	**0.99**	**3.51**	**2.23**	**0.60**

Source: Malkamäki and Vesala (1996).

Moreover, banks seem to have underestimated the increased risks attributable to changed bank-customer relationships and risks involved in asset-based lending.

Banks entered the 1980s poorly capitalized in terms of book or market value. The insufficient cushion against loan losses made banks vulnerable to adverse economic shocks and gave them a strong incentive for risk taking to maximize the option value of deposit insurance.[29]

In Finland and Norway, the book-value ratio of shareholder equity to total assets of all banks ranged from 2 percent to 2½ percent. The financial strength of the Norwegian banking industry was further weakened because banks were allowed to count subordinated debt as equity capital. By 1990, the subordinated debt of Norwegian commercial banks represented about three-quarters of their equity capital. The Swedish banks also had low capital ratios, in the range of 3½–4½ percent; however, the banks had accumulated substantial loan loss reserves, which were tax deductible.

In principle, leverage-related and risk-related costs (such as bankruptcy costs) may restrain banks' incentive to take risks, as can regulatory costs that potentially change with the riskiness of a bank's portfolio and capitalization (see Shrieves and Dahl, 1992). Taken together, however, the reduced regulatory costs that were associated with deregulation and the low equity ratios provided a strong incentive for banks to accommodate the surge in credit demand and to bear more risk.

The trend toward riskier lending could also have resulted from the diminished franchise values of deposit banks as a consequence of deregulation and increased competition.[30] Before the mid-1980s, banks in Finland, Norway, and Sweden operated in highly regulated markets that tended to thwart competition and allow banks to earn considerable economic rents (excess profits) from providing financial services. But instead of the rents benefiting shareholders, banks appear to have used them to boost the scale of their operations.[31] This was particularly apparent in Finland and Norway, where an extensive branch network, high operating costs, and low profits prevailed. In principle, deregulation reduces future bank profitability and thus tends to lower rents in the banking industry. Given the rigid cost structure and reduced scope for discretionary expenditures, bank managers in Finland, Norway, and Sweden, like shareholders, had to take on increased risk to get higher returns after financial liberalization.

Fearing that they could lose ground in the vigorous competition touched off by liberalization, many banks, in particular some large ones, pursued aggressive lending policies as a preemptive response and were prepared to accept higher risk. In this context, the aggressive lending behavior of the Finnish savings banks following a loss of market share in the early 1980s may not be surprising in hindsight. They probably faced the biggest scope for risk taking on account of their ownership structure—they can be characterized as managerially controlled banks without shareholders to monitor behavior. Moreover, savings banks shared their credit risks through a system of mutual loan insurance. Given that individual institutions accordingly did not bear the entire default risk, this system potentially created a strong incentive to grant risky loans. To what extent the scope for risk taking was actually used, however, depended on bank management, as illustrated by the Finnish cooperative banks. Although cooperative banks shared many structural characteristics of savings banks, including mutual loan insurance, they pursued more cautious lending policies.

Beyond changing incentives, financial liberalization also altered traditional banking relations, with adverse implications for banks' ability to monitor the creditworthiness of customers. Before deregulation, close relationships existed between banks and their borrowers owing to credit rationing. After market forces became dominant in the credit market, transaction-based banking gained more importance relative to relationship banking. In that connection, banks appear to have underestimated the increased risk of the larger pools of borrowers to whom they were lending. Moreover, banks' internal credit poli-

---

[29]The incentive for bank risk taking tends to rise as the relative share of equity financing declines. See, for example, Furlong and Keeley (1989). In Finland, deposit insurance funds have been in existence for savings and cooperative banks since the 1930s and for commercial banks since the 1960s; deposit insurance was made mandatory in 1969. Insurance coverage is unlimited. The insurance funds are operated by their member banks and charge a flat-rate premium. Their resources, however, proved inadequate for the banking crisis.

[30]A related hypothesis on the impact of liberalization on bank risk taking focuses on the erosion of rents accruing to shareholders. This argument has been applied to U.S. bank performance by Keeley (1990) and Fries (1993). For a discussion of this hypothesis in the context of the Nordic countries, see Llewellyn (1992).

---

[31]Economic rents accruing to shareholders can be measured by the ratio of the market value to the book value of their assets (Tobin's q ratio). See Keeley (1990) and Fries (1993) for an application to the banking industry. The basic premise behind this measure is that the capitalized value of any excess profits is reflected in the market value but not the book value of bank assets. For selected banks in Finland, Norway, and, Sweden, Tobin's q ratios were not significantly higher than 1 before financial liberalization, which points to the absence of excess profits accruing to shareholders.

cies and control mechanisms appear to have been inadequate for the task of assessing credit risks and of monitoring debtors in the newly deregulated environment. In Finnish and Swedish commercial banks, complicated cross shareholdings with nonfinancial corporations provided ample opportunity for connected lending, and credit exposures often exceeded prudent limits.[32] Although significant interest rate risks were shifted to the borrower because most loans carried variable interest rates, banks did not adequately anticipate the possibility that a surge in interest rates could turn a borrower's interest rate risk into the bank's credit risk, as demonstrated in Finland and Sweden in the early 1990s when monetary conditions were sharply tightened.

The experience in the Nordic countries also illustrates the potential pitfalls of asset-based lending. Banks appear to have misjudged the initial upward pressure on asset prices as a sustained trend justified by favorable fundamentals. With the steady and often spectacular increases in prices, banks were prepared in some cases to provide almost 100 percent financing for asset purchases, requiring only that the asset serve as collateral. Some borrowers had inadequate equity stakes leaving the banks vulnerable to an economic downturn and asset price deflation.[33]

Policymakers' Response

The response by policymakers was inadequate for three reasons. The authorities failed to see the need to tighten prudential bank regulation in areas such as real estate and foreign currency lending; the favorable tax treatment of interest payments was not reformed until well after the credit boom; and monetary conditions were not tightened sufficiently and in a timely manner.

It is now widely recognized that economic deregulation needs to be supplemented by a strengthening of prudential regulations (see Bisat, Johnston, and Sundararajan, 1992; Sundararajan and Baliño, 1991; and White, 1991). But in the Nordic countries little emphasis was placed at the time of deregulation on strengthening and adapting prudential safety-and-soundness regulations to the new competitive environment, in particular in the areas of real estate and foreign currency lending. Even after deregulation, the bank supervisory offices in the Nordic countries

continued to focus primarily on the banks' compliance with regulation and did not review in depth the banks' lending practices and risk-management policies. Furthermore, at the height of the credit expansion by banks, the banking supervisory offices in Norway and Sweden were merged with the insurance supervisory bodies and devoted special attention to developing capital markets and less attention to monitoring the banking system. In Finland and Norway, routine on-site inspections—rather than being increased—were sharply reduced as a result of the explicit move toward document-based supervision. In Finland, direct supervision and on-site inspections of savings and cooperative banks remained the sole responsibility of their own supervisory bodies.

With high marginal tax rates, the tax deductibility of interest expenses meant that the real cost of borrowing for households was low during most of the 1980s; the real costs of purchasing a home were in fact markedly negative. Yet, mainly for political reasons, the authorities did not correct these incentives at the time of deregulation; instead, tax reforms were delayed until 1988 in Norway (when marginal tax rates were lowered) and 1990–91 in Finland and Sweden (when marginal tax rates were lowered and the deductibility of interest payments was curtailed).[34]

Despite the sharp growth in lending and the surge in private indebtedness, monetary conditions were not immediately tightened. Norges Bank sharply increased central bank credit to banks, from 3 percent to 23 percent of the private credit extended by banks in 1986, following the 10 percent devaluation of the Norwegian krone that was triggered by a decline in oil prices.[35] The increase in the banks' borrowing facility was a deliberate measure to offset an anticipated decline in foreign borrowing (which never materialized). In Finland, the exchange rate peg initially constrained the monetary policy response, but in early 1989 the markka was revalued by 4 percent and a special reserve requirement was imposed to slow the growth in bank lending. Yet some banks, in particular savings banks, chose to pay the penalty rates instead of curtailing their lending growth (see Nyberg and Vihriälä, 1994).

---

[32]The Finnish Deposit Bank Act of 1991 introduced exposure limits.

[33]High leverage itself may also have contributed to an adverse selection problem among borrowers (see Stiglitz, 1993).

[34]The Swedish tax reform lowered to 30 percent the share of interest expenses that could be deducted from the taxable income of households (Bank Support Authority, 1993). In Finland, the deductibility was reduced in steps between 1990 and 1993.

[35]At the end of 1987, central bank financing accounted for 28 percent of the commercial banks' total assets and 14 percent of savings banks' total assets.

V Boom-and-Bust Cycles and the Banking Crises

In the previous section, we discussed the response of borrowers, lenders, and policymakers to deregulation; we now turn to the macroeconomic environment that developed following deregulation. All three countries experienced a pronounced long-lived boom-and-bust cycle. Against that background, we will argue that financial liberalization and the accommodative macroeconomic policies contributed significantly to the economic boom, but at the same time made the economies more susceptible to macroeconomic shocks as long as economic agents had not fully adjusted their behavior to the new regulatory environment.

Boom-and-Bust Cycles

The economic boom followed a similar pattern in the three countries (see Jonung, Soderstrom, and Stymne, 1994). The initial impulse came from abroad when exports rose, such as in Norway following the oil price hike in the early 1980s, or when the terms of trade improved significantly in Finland and Sweden after the oil price decline in 1986 and the surge in world market prices for paper and pulp products in the late 1980s. These initial effects spilled over strongly into domestic demand. In particular, private consumption rose sharply as employment and incomes rose; the initial stimulus was amplified by easier access to credit after the deregulation and by rising wealth attributable to higher asset prices. As a result, the household saving rate in Norway and Sweden became negative. The domestic boom, which was characterized by sharply higher investment activity, was also reinforced by the rapid expansion of credit that fueled speculation in shares and real estate, which in turn raised wealth levels and thus made additional borrowing possible. Monetary policy options to limit the expansionary effects of deregulation were, however, constrained by fixed exchange rate regimes and fiscal policies do not appear to have been tight enough.

In Norway, the downturn was experienced earlier than in the other two countries because of Norway's heavy dependency on oil exports. The negative terms of trade shock that resulted from the sharp decline in oil prices in 1986, however, did not immediately cause a recession in Norway, and lending growth persisted, aided in part by the additional liquidity support provided by the central bank to financial institutions following the devaluation in 1986.

By the late 1980s, it became increasingly clear also in Finland and Sweden that neither the upward trend in asset prices, which was in part driven by expectations of high inflation, nor the favorable macroeconomic conditions would last and that much of the recent borrowing had pushed private indebtedness to unsustainable heights. The tax reforms in the Nordic countries, in combination with a tightening of monetary policy and lower inflation, raised real after-tax lending rates noticeably and contributed to the sharp drop in property and bank share prices (Figure 7). In response, households began to consolidate their financial positions by cutting back on consumption, and businesses decreased investment considerably. As a result, all three Nordic countries entered a deep recession that in turn accelerated the asset price deflation. Compounding the initial domestic demand shock was the collapse of trade with the member countries of the Council for Mutual Economic Assistance in 1990–91, which affected Finland in particular, and the drop in paper and pulp prices in the world market.

In addition, the depreciation of the Norwegian krone in 1986, the Finnish markka in 1991–93, and the Swedish krona in 1992 increased the domestic currency value of debt denominated in foreign currency. This increase was significant for Finland and Sweden because, in the late 1980s, more than half of the borrowing by the corporate sector was denominated in foreign currency (Brunilla and Takala, 1993). The depreciation was particularly burdensome for firms in the sheltered sectors that lacked foreign currency earnings.[36] In general, it became increasingly difficult for small and medium-sized firms to gain access to outside financing. In some

---

[36]In fact, almost half of the foreign currency loans had been extended to the domestic sector.

Figure 7. Price Indicators
(1980 = 100)

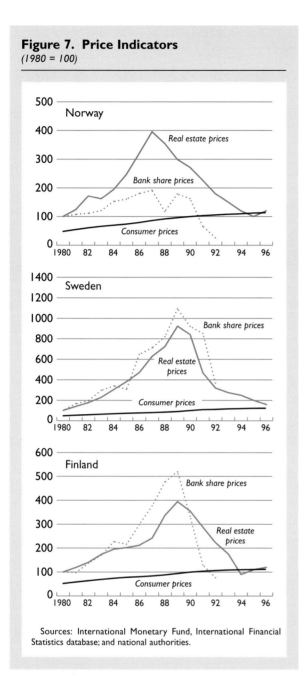

Sources: International Monetary Fund, International Financial Statistics database; and national authorities.

in collateral values thus quickly translated into losses in the financial sector that led to the banking crises.

Banking Crises

Both in Norway and Sweden, finance companies were the first to show the effects of the emerging crisis in 1986–87 and 1990–91, respectively. Their losses—mainly from property investments—exceeded 5 percent of loans, and many of them went out of business or were restructured. With a one-year lag, it became clear that the difficulties of the finance companies had spilled over to banks because of their involvement in finance companies.

The problems that emerged in the first phase of the Norwegian crisis (1988–89), including heavy loan losses, were regarded as mainly due to bad banking and excessive lending by some small and medium-sized banks. They were not considered a threat to the solidity of the Norwegian banking industry as a whole. Loan losses, however, unexpectedly surged in 1991 to 6 percent of GDP as more banks, including several of the largest, encountered financial difficulties. In 1992, the household and corporate sectors accounted for 20 percent and 77 percent of these losses, respectively (Table 11). In contrast to the first phase of the crisis in 1988 and 1989, when primarily newly established firms faced problems, in 1991 well-established firms, especially in the trade, hotels and restaurants, and real estate sectors, defaulted on their loans (Commission on the Banking Crisis, 1992).

For Swedish bank groups as a whole, nonperforming loans increased to 11 percent of GDP in 1993. A relatively small share of the credit losses (11 percent) was attributable to households, while the bulk (75 percent) concerned nonfinancial enterprises. Foreign loans accounted for about 9 percent of loan losses. Initially, the situation of banks was dominated by the real estate crisis: real-estate-related losses accounted for 75 percent of total loan losses in 1991 and about 50 percent in 1993. However, as the recession deepened, the proportion of nonperforming loans not connected with real estate grew substantially.[37]

In Finland, nonperforming bank loans rose sharply in 1992 to 9.3 percent of banks' total exposure, even after 3.7 percent had been written off as loan and guarantee losses (see Pensala and Solttila, 1993, for more information). In 1993, almost 60 percent of the loan losses were accounted for by firms, while households

cases, even viable firms faced bankruptcies because they were unable to ease liquidity problems through new borrowing. Bankruptcy rates reached record levels in all three countries; in Norway, the number of corporate bankruptcies rose by 40 percent a year during 1986–89 (Figure 8). The financial problems of highly indebted corporate and private borrowers led to a sharp rise in banks' nonperforming loans. The accumulation of losses and repayment difficulties in the nonfinancial sector as well as the decline

---

[37]The decline in the share of real-estate-related nonperforming loans is mainly due to the conversion of some of these loans into real estate holdings by banks.

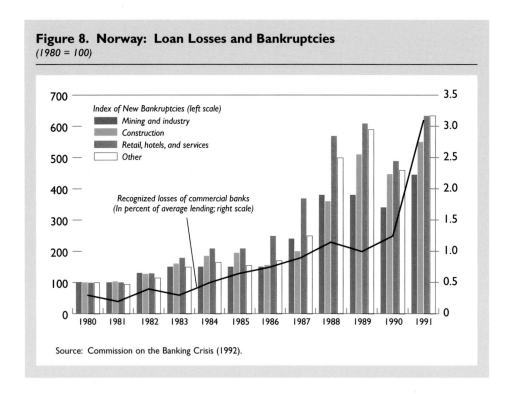

Figure 8. Norway: Loan Losses and Bankruptcies
(1980 = 100)

Index of New Bankruptcies (left scale)
- Mining and industry
- Construction
- Retail, hotels, and services
- Other

Recognized losses of commercial banks
(In percent of average lending; right scale)

Source: Commission on the Banking Crisis (1992).

were responsible for 25 percent (Table 11). The largest default rates were in the services, real estate and the construction sectors; almost half of banks' real estate exposure was either written off as credit losses or was nonperforming in 1992. The same was true for con-struction loans in 1993. In contrast, less than 1 percent of loans to households were booked as credit losses in 1992 and 1993.

An analysis of financial ratios based on bank balance sheets and income statements reveals some

Table 11. Nonperforming Loans
(In percent of total loans)

	Norway		Sweden		Finland	
	1988	1992	1991	1993	1991	1993
Firms	80	77	84	75	59	58
Of which:						
Industry	19	6	n.a.	n.a.	9	8
Construction	5	8	n.a.	n.a.	10	12
Trade, restaurants, hotels	24	25	n.a.	n.a.	13	14
Real estate business	16	30	75	50	16	12
Domestic financial institutions	n.a.	7	15	3	n.a.	n.a.
Other	16	8	n.a.	n.a.	11	12
Households	15	20	7	11	21	25
Foreign borrowers	n.a.	n.a.	5	9	14	12
Other	5	3	4	5	6	5

Sources: Commission on the Banking Crisis (1992); Norges Bank; Sveriges Riksbank; and Bank of Finland.

Table 12. Selected Financial Ratios for Commercial Banks
(In percent of total assets)

| | Banks Subject to Official Intervention[1] | | | | Banks Not Subject to Official Intervention | | | |
| | Norway | | Finland | Sweden | Norway | | Finland | Sweden |
	1989	1991	1991	1991	1989	1991	1991	1991
Loans to public	87.80	90.20	52.10	78.0	61.50	68.20	51.97	47.0
Deposits from public	58.30	54.10	20.30	49.0	53.20	61.30	33.14	38.0
Loans from central bank	26.90	27.40	0.74	11.0	10.10	12.20	0.78	4.0
Equity capital	−5.00	1.90	3.86	4.1	5.10	6.60	6.22	7.6
Net interest income	3.64	2.70	−0.48	—	3.48	3.34	1.26	—
Operating profits before losses	0.49	−0.03	0.07	0.7	1.79	1.40	0.51	2.30
Operating profits after realized losses	−8.25	−4.93	−2.87	−10.4	0.09	−0.89	−0.59	−0.40

Source: IMF staff calculations.

[1]Official intervention is defined as a case where capital is judged inadequate by the regulators and the institution is closed, merged out of existence, taken over by the government, or sold through purchase-and-assumption agreements. Financial ratios were calculated for the period just prior to intervention

common trends. Table 12 presents some financial ratios for commercial banks that were classified officially as insolvent compared with those that remained solvent. The data reveal that failed institutions funded a larger proportion of their loans through sources other than deposits, in particular through money markets and foreign borrowing. This type of funding carried higher costs and meant higher exposure to foreign exchange risks. In addition, as far as Norway is concerned, liquidity provided by the central bank played a much larger role for failed institutions.

Because the Nordic banks, in particular Finnish and Norwegian banks, entered the recession with a relatively small capital base, the huge credit losses eroded the banks' equity positions quickly. As a result of problem assets, bank profitability deteriorated sharply in all three countries, and income from financial operations declined on account of the loss of interest payments on nonperforming assets.

VI Bank Restructuring Operations and the Performance of the Banking Systems

It is generally considered important that a banking crisis be resolved quickly to minimize the adverse effects that arise from distorted incentives caused by the operation of insolvent financial institutions. Depending on the nature of the crisis, the authorities can apply a number of support measures. An injection of short-term liquidity into the affected banks would be sufficient in a mere liquidity crisis. In circumstances such as the Nordic banking crises that are characterized by widespread solvency problems, a more active government role is usually required. In such situations, authorities face the choice of providing capital to a troubled bank without any change in its ownership and operation (sometimes referred to as "open-bank assistance"), or taking the bank over and runing it as a publicly owned institution. Alternatively, the government may choose either to liquidate the insolvent bank and pay off depositors and other creditors (not necessarily in full) or to sell the troubled bank through a so-called purchase and assumption agreement. Regardless of which specific method of bank support is chosen, the incentives that accompany government bank support should be analyzed carefully to minimize the overall costs of the operation and to keep the distortions created by government intervention small.

In all three Nordic countries, the government and, to some extent, the central bank supported the banking systems. The government took over a number of large banks but only a very few (and mostly small) banks were liquidated. In the majority of cases, the authorities either assumed ownership (most often with the intention of finding a buyer for the bank in the near to medium term) or provided funds (mainly as equity injections) to banks that continued to operate as private institutions. Governments provided this direct support—in particular immediately after the crises broke—in the form of net worth certificates, promissory notes, and other forms of injection of capital, as well as by assuming debt or through guarantees to a bank without revoking its charter. This type of bank support can be controversial because it may imply subsidizing the bank's current shareholders by allowing the bank to continue to operate even though it may be insolvent. It is possible that such government assistance has terms (such as interest rates) attached that are below market. Guarantees are particularly difficult to price accurately. More generally, open-bank assistance can entail a form of subsidization that can noticeably distort competition among financial institutions.

In Finland and Sweden, nonperforming bank assets were in many cases lifted into asset-management companies; such arrangements were not utilized in Norway. The main objective for separating nonperforming assets from the viable part of a bank is to correct risk-taking incentives. Another argument in favor of transferring nonperforming assets to a separate agency lies in the fact that it is a once-and-for-all solution because the remaining healthy bank should be able to manage without further government involvement. In general, an asset-management company may represent less direct involvement for the government than an injection of capital or a guarantee of nonperforming assets. Moreover, a specialized institution that deals exclusively with the sale of nonperforming assets may be more efficient in recovering the maximum possible value due to economies of scale and specific expertise. However, it can also be argued that a private institution, such as an acquiring bank that shares in the proceeds of the sale of the bad assets, may have an even stronger incentive to maximize the recovery effort than a government-run agency.

In Norway, two separate agencies, the Government Bank Insurance Fund and the Government Bank Investment Fund, were set up in 1991 to deal with the banking problems. The former provided support mainly through the banks' own deposit insurance funds and the latter through direct capital investment in banks. Support from the banks' own deposit insurance funds was most substantial in Norway, where the funds contributed about one-third of bank support resources. In Finland, the corresponding contribution to savings and commercial banks was small, but the deposit insurance fund of the cooperative bank provided considerable support.

Unlike the Norwegian central bank, the Swedish central bank did not directly participate in the support of financial institutions. Although the Bank of

Finland played the lead role in the early stages of the crisis, the bulk of bank support was provided either directly by the government or by the Government Guarantee Fund.

Overall, the Finnish banks have received substantially more support than the other Nordic banks. The direct fiscal impact of bank support operations has been relatively small in Norway at 2.6 percent of GDP compared with 5.2 percent of GDP in Sweden and 10 percent of GDP in Finland. Unlike the Finnish and Swedish governments, the Norwegian government did not issue a general and public guarantee of banks' commitments. Instead, the government handled the Norwegian banking crisis by a quick takeover of the three largest commercial banks.

The Norwegian Experience

In the first phase of the Norwegian banking crisis (1988–89), the two industry-operated deposit insurance funds—the Commercial Banks Guarantee Fund and the Savings Banks Guarantee Fund—assisted a number of ailing banks and provided funds to facilitate mergers with stronger banks.[38]

Toward the end of 1990, accumulated bank losses had virtually exhausted the capital of the deposit insurance funds, and it became clear that the funds would not be able to meet the banking industry's increasing capital needs.[39] To shore up confidence in the banking system the government established a new fund in March 1991—the Government Bank Insurance Fund. Its objective was to provide loans to the Commercial and Savings Banks Guarantee Funds to enable them to supply capital to individual member banks.[40] To receive support, the beneficiary bank was required to present a business plan designed to improve operating profits and reduce its risk-weighted assets. In most cases, the support was conditional on the implementation of cost-cutting measures.

To deal with the crisis, the Norwegian parliament adopted several new measures in November 1991 that were intended to reinforce the guarantee system, raise bank profitability, and accelerate the recapitalization of ailing banks. These measures included:

(1) An increase of NKr 6 billion in the capital of the Government Bank Insurance Fund.

(2) The extension of the mandate of the Government Bank Insurance Fund to allow it to provide distressed banks with Tier 1 capital.

(3) A budgetary allocation of NKr 1 billion to the Savings Banks Guarantee Fund.

(4) The creation of the Government Bank Investment Fund, with a capital of NKr 4.5 billion. Its objective was to participate on commercial terms and together with private investors in bank equity issues.

The government's stake in the commercial banking system was to be managed by the Government Bank Insurance Fund, which was established as a short-term facility, and the Government Bank Investment Fund, which was assigned to manage long-term state investment in the banking sector. The government planed to wind down the operations of the Government Bank Insurance Fund by 2000–2002, when the Commercial Banks Guarantee Fund was expected to be fully reconstituted. To this end, procedures have been established for the eventual transfer of the Government Bank Insurance Fund's liquid assets to the treasury and the sale of its commercial bank shareholdings to the Government Bank Investment Fund. In contrast, the Government Bank Investment Fund had an indefinite mandate to secure a substantial element of national ownership in Norwegian banks. By maintaining indefinitely at least a one-third interest in the two largest commercial banks, the government intended to ensure, first, that the focus of these banks remained on financing Norwegian industry and, second, that the imprudent lending that contributed to the banking crisis would not be repeated.

Bank Support Measures

A small commercial bank, Norion Bank, which was founded in 1987 and pursued an aggressive asset growth strategy, was placed under public administration in 1989, and was liquidated after interim accounts indicated that its share capital was lost. All bank depositors received full compensation one week after the bank was closed, which was facilitated by a loan from Norges Bank and a guarantee from the Commercial Banks Guarantee Fund.

In August 1991, the Government Bank Insurance Fund provided the Commercial Banks Guarantee Fund with two support loans totaling NKr 2,450 million (Table 13, footnote 4). The loans were used to

---

[38]Funds relied on deposit insurance contributions by banks.

[39]At the end of 1990, the Commercial Banks Guarantee Fund's capital was NKr 3.8 billion. However, in December 1990, the Commercial Banks Guarantee Fund had provided Fokus Bank with an equity capital guarantee of NKr 1.5 billion for which it had not made provisions, and it had set a quota of NKr 2 billion for the supply of preference capital to member banks. Thus, the scope for the Commercial Banks Guarantee Fund to provide additional support funds was severely constrained. The Savings Bank Guarantee Fund, for its part, had guarantee liabilities of NKr 1.2 billion, but capital of only NKr 38 million at book value (Wilse, 1995).

[40]The interest charged on the loans to the Commercial Banks Guarantee Fund or Savings Banks Guarantee Fund was to correspond to that on the government's account in Norges Bank.

Table 13. Norway: Funds Used in Rescue Operations[1]
(In millions of Norwegian kroner)

		Savings Banks Guarantee Fund		Commercial Banks Guarantee Fund	Government Bank Insurance Fund		Government Bank Investment Fund	
Year	Bank	Guarantee	Equity	Equity	Guarantee	Equity		
1988	Sparebanken Nord-Norge	600			200			
1989	Sparebanken Nord-Norge	650	1, 456		500			
	Sunnmorsbanken			580				
	Norion Bank			305	73			
	Other savings banks	73	288					
1990	Sparebanken Nord-Norge	650	7					
	Sunnmorsbanken			466				
	Other savings banks	567	172					
1991	Den Norske Bank			940				
	Fokus Bank			2,150[2]			475	
	Christiania Bank			2,724			5,140	
	Sparebanken Midt-Norge		525					
	Sparebanken Rogaland		600					
	Sparebanken Nord-Norge	800						
	Oslobanken							63
	Other commercial banks			22				20
	Other savings banks	138	504					
1992[1]	Den Norske Bank					600	4,750	1,675
	Christiania Bank						1,900	
	Sparebanken Midt-Norge		75			200	600	
	Sparebanken Rogaland		144					
	Other savings banks							1,070
	Total	3,478	3,768[3]	7,187[4]	773	800	12,865	2,828

Sources: Commission on the Banking Crisis (1992); Organization for Economic Cooperation and Development (1995).
[1]No official support was provided to banks after 1992.
[2]Indicates also subordinate convertible debt.
[3]Indicates NKr 539 million made on the basis of support loans from the Government Bank Insurance Fund.
[4]Includes NKr 2.45 billion made on the basis of support loans from the Government Bank Insurance Fund.

inject preference capital into Christiania Bank and Fokus Bank to allow them to meet the statutory capital adequacy requirements.[41] Furthermore, in October 1991, the Government Bank Insurance Fund supplied the Savings Bank Guarantee Fund with NKr 320 million in support loans that, in conjunction with a NKr 1 billion allocation from the government, was used to finance NKr 1,125 million capital injection to Sparebanken Midt-Norge and Sparebanken Rogaland. As a result, by the end of October 1991, the Government Bank Insurance Fund had disbursed NKr 2,770 million, over half of its capital, in support loans.

[41]At the same time, the Commercial Banks Guarantee Fund provided a further NKr 300 million of its own resources to Christiania Bank.

It became clear that the three largest commercial banks, Den Norske, Christiania, and Fokus, which together held 85 percent of total commercial bank assets, were in greater difficulty than previously thought. Christiania and Fokus had negative equity capital positions after their share capital and a sizable portion of preference capital were written off. Den Norske applied for an infusion of preference capital in October and November 1991 when it became clear that it was unable to raise capital in the private market.

The direct fiscal impact of the banking crisis in terms of funds used in rescue operations during 1991–92 amounted to about NKr 19.2 billion (2.6 percent of GDP) (Table 13). The bulk of these funds (NKr 17.8 billion) was allocated to the three largest banks (Den Norske, Christiania, and Fokus) to enable them to meet the capital requirements, which was crucial if Norwegian banks were to maintain foreign financing and international creditworthiness. By the end of 1991, the government had become the sole owner or the majority shareholder of the three largest commercial banks, accounting for about 85 percent of the total assets of all commercial banks.[42]

The Swedish Experience

In Sweden, the first bank to face problems was Nordbanken, the third-largest bank at the time. (For more details, see Bank Support Authority, 1993.) Because the state was the major owner of the bank in late 1991, it ended up subscribing SKr 4.2 billion (0.5 percent of GDP) of a SKr 5.1 billion new share issue that it had guaranteed. New management was appointed immediately. One year later, the government purchased all minority share holdings. In return for the transfer of nonperforming assets to Securum AB (an asset-management company), Nordbanken received an additional capital injection of SKr 10 billion (1 percent of GDP).

By mid-1992, the government explicitly recognized that it needed a coherent strategy to deal with the crisis. Its overriding concern was to avoid a systemic collapse of the banking system and to avert the loss of foreign lines of credit. It therefore chose a centralized approach to providing assistance. In September 1992, the government announced that it would guarantee that all bank commitments be met on a timely basis and that no depositors, creditors, or other parties would suffer any losses (see Bank Support Authority, 1993). Subsequent legislation confirmed the guarantee; only share capital and perpetual debentures were excluded from the guarantee. The government was authorized to provide support flexibly in the form of loan guarantees, capital contributions, and other appropriate measures. There was no upper limit on the amount that could be spent on support operations.

The Bank Support Act (December 1992) stipulated that the long-term fiscal costs should be minimized and that paid-out support should be recovered to the fullest extent possible. Moreover, it was explicitly stated that the government should not endeavor to assume ownership of banks and credit institutions. Rather, the blanket guarantee scheme was considered to be exceptional and temporary; in fact,

it was actually repealed by the parliament and replaced by a limited deposit insurance scheme on July 1, 1996.

To support the objectives of the act, parliament set up a separate agency, the Bank Support Authority, to manage the support system and decide on measures. The authority was only set up formally in May 1993 when banks had started to recover and most of the restructuring was completed. In 1996, the Bank Support Authority was reduced to a dormant body with one permanent employee.

Bank Support Measures

Unlike many other countries, where special government bond issues were exchanged for nonperforming bank loans, Sweden's main form of assistance consisted of the guarantee of banks' liabilities, which were to be financed from the budget as required. From late 1992, such assistance was offered to the entire banking system. Although several of the major banks availed themselves of these guarantees, nearly 98 percent of all the state's assistance was given to two large banks (Nordbanken and Gota Bank) and their associated asset-management companies (Table 14).

In the spring of 1992, it became clear that Nordbanken was in serious difficulty. To facilitate restructuring, the state bought all outstanding shares (for about SKr 2 billion) and then split the bank into a "good bank" and an asset-management company. The asset-management company, Securum, took over the bad assets, with a book value of SKr 67 billion, while Nordbanken was left with the performing assets. In addition, the state provided Nordbanken and Securum with equity capital (SKr 10 billion and 24 billion, respectively) and gave Securum SKr 10 billion in loan guarantees.

By September 1991, Gota Bank (the fourth largest bank) was incurring losses at a rate such that it would not meet the capital adequacy requirement at year-end and was in danger of becoming insolvent. To bolster confidence in the banking sector and safeguard the payments system, the government decided to meet all the commitments of Gota Bank, but not those of the parent company, Gota AB, which was declared bankrupt. The government assumed full ownership of Gota Bank at no cost (following arbitration, the value of the shares was declared to be zero). During 1993, two guarantees against losses were provided while the bank was being restructured. The reconstruction involved transferring the nonperforming loans to a specially created asset-management company, Retriva AB, which was endowed by the government with equity capital of SKr 3.8 billion. Nordbanken and Gota Bank received 98 percent of the budgetary assistance, but the

---

[42]By December 1992, the state-run Government Insurance Fund was sole owner of Fokus Bank and owned 98 percent of the shares in Christiania Bank. The state also owned 55 percent of the shares of Den Norske Bank through the Government Bank Investment Fund.

Table 14. Sweden: Funds Used in Rescue Operations[1]

(In millions of Swedish kronor)

	Total Commitment	Paid Out	Charged to the State's Budget
Savings bank foundations			
Guarantees[1]	6,803	—	—
Interest subsidies	1,028	1,028	1,028
Total	7,831	1,028	1,028
Nordbanken			
Share subscription 1991	4,191	4,181	4,191
Share purchase 1992	2,055	2,065	2,055
Capital contribution 1992	10,000	10,000	10,000
Total	16,246	16,246	16,246
Securum			
Guarantee 1992[2]	9,850	9,850	9,850
Guarantee 1992[3]	13,150	13,150	13,150
Share purchase 1993	1,000	1,000	—
Guarantee 1993	10,000	—	—
Total	34,000	24,000	23,000
Gota Bank			
Capital contribution 1993	20,000	20,000	20,000
Guarantee shareholder's equity[4]	231	231	231
Total	20,231	20,231	20,231
Retriva			
Capital contribution 1993	3,800	3,800	—
Guarantee 1993	3,500	—	—
Total	7,300	3,800	—
Föreningsbanken			
Capital adequacy protection 1993	2,500	—	—
Total bank support[5]	88,108	65,305	60,505

Sources: Swedish Banking Association; Ministry of Finance; Bank Support Authority (1996).

[1]No official support was provided to banks after 1993.

[2]At the time of the agreement, the guarantee to the savings bank foundations was about SKr 5.5 billion, calculated at present value.

[3]The guarantee to Securum has declined by SKr 1 billion, through Securum working this claim after propagation of the 1993 year-end financial statements.

[4]The prior guarantee of SKr 3 billion of shareholders' equity in Gota Bank to Nordbanken was discharged in an amount of SKr 231 million after the year-end financial statements were approved.

[5]In addition to the above charges of SKr 60,586 million against the national budget, the appropriations to strengthen the financial system were charged with a further SKr 2,722 million.

government also provided financial support to Sparbanken Sverige and extended large guarantees to other banks that, in the event, were not used.

In 1993, Nordbanken and Gota Bank were merged, retaining the name Nordbanken, and became Sweden's fourth-largest bank. The two asset-management companies that were created to deal with the banks' nonperforming loans, Securum and Retriva, were merged in December 1995.

Total commitments (including guarantees) amounted to SKr 85 billion (5.9 percent of GDP). However, because not all guarantees were paid out, budgetary support mainly took the form of capital injections (86 percent), with lesser amounts provided

by share subscriptions or share purchases (10 percent) and interest subsidies (2 percent). The direct cost to the budget was SKr 61 billion (4.2 percent of GDP). Moreover, the net fiscal cost has been diminishing over time, as the asset-management companies have been recovering loan losses and the state has reduced its bank ownership. In October 1995, the government sold 34.5 percent of its ownership stake in Nordbanken for SKr 6.4 billion (0.4 percent of GDP). The value of the government's remaining equity in Nordbanken was estimated in mid-1996 to be about SKr 17 billion (1 percent of GDP). In contrast to the expectations in 1993, when the SKr 24 billion injections were expected to be written off over

15 years, it is now widely anticipated that 40–50 percent of the original equity capital will be recovered (0.6 percent of GDP).

The two asset-management companies, Securum and Retriva, have been quite successful in liquidating their assets and have recovered substantial amounts. After the merger and further reorganization, Nordbanken has become the most profitable bank in Sweden. The cost of the crisis has been estimated at 4 percent of GDP in cash and 6 percent including guarantees. Asset recovery and privatization receipts have reduced the cash outlays to an estimated 2.1 percent of GDP.

The Finnish Experience

Finnish bank support has been channeled through three organizations: the Bank of Finland, a newly established Government Guarantee Fund, and the state budget (see Nyberg and Vihriälä, 1994, for details on Finnish bank support measures). At first, the Bank of Finland was the only institution in a position to rescue a bank, such as Skopbank in late 1991. After the Skopbank experience had revealed the need for a new agency to deal with the spreading banking crisis, the Government Guarantee Fund (GGF) was established in April 1992.[43] Developments in 1992, however, demonstrated that the administration of bank support was inadequate. The GGF had no full-time staff of its own, and it was recognized that a conflict of interest could arise from the representation of the Bank of Finland and the Banking Supervision Office on the GGF's executive board. The Guarantee Fund in turn was accountable to a parliamentary committee. According to the new organizational structure, which was approved in February 1993, only the Ministry of Finance was represented on the GGF board. Moreover, the GGF now reported directly to the government, which would in the future decide on all bank support measures, rather than the GGF. In connection with the GGF's reorganization, parliament unanimously approved a resolution that reaffirmed the authorities' commitment to guarantee that Finnish banks were able to meet their commitments on time under all circumstances.

As a further step to improve financial supervision, the Banking Supervision Office, which had been part of the Ministry of Finance, became an autonomous unit within the Bank of Finland and was renamed the Financial Supervision Authority (see Aranko, 1994). At the same time, its responsibilities were extended to foreign exchange risk, an area that had previously been assigned to the Bank of Finland.

Bank Support Measures

The savings bank sector had been particularly hit by the banking crisis. A liquidity crisis in September 1991 prompted the Bank of Finland—at the time the only government agency equipped to conduct a rescue operation—to take over Skopbank. Two asset-management companies were formed: one took possession of Skopbank's industrial holdings, while the other took over the real estate holdings. Bank management was replaced, and a plan was drafted to reduce Skopbank's balance sheet and operating costs. As part of the rescue operation, the Bank of Finland committed about Fmk 14 billion in 1991 and 1992 (Table 15). In June 1992, the Guarantee Fund acquired Skopbank from the Bank of Finland for Fmk 1.4 billion, while the holding companies managing Skopbank's former corporate holdings and real estate investments remained with the Bank of Finland. By 1994, Skopbank had received Fmk 15.2 billion (3 percent of GDP) in bank support: Fmk 9.8 billion from the Bank of Finland, Fmk 4 billion from the Guarantee Fund, and Fmk 1.4 billion from the state budget. The loan and guarantee portfolio of Skopbank and its subsidiaries, Skop Finance Ltd. and Industrialization Fund Ltd., were sold to Sweden's Handelsbanken in June 1992. Skopbank continued to operate as a commercial bank and to serve the remaining savings banks as their central bank.

In early 1992, several savings banks developed financial problems, partly because of their stakes in Skopbank, but mainly as a result of their own aggressive lending in 1988 and 1989. Because savings banks were closely interconnected by a mutual solvency insurance scheme, a total of 41 savings banks (problem and nonproblem banks) were merged into the Savings Bank of Finland, which was subsequently taken over by the GGF.[44] In the process, the savings bank foundations lost their equity stakes in the merged banks. The Guarantee Fund provided a capital injection of Fmk 5.5 billion and subordinated debt worth Fmk 1.4 billion. In December 1992, an extra Fmk 4.7 billion was provided as capital to cover larger-than-expected write-offs of nonperforming real estate loans. At the same time, the Savings Bank of Finland was converted into a joint stock

---

[43]The fund was initially endowed with Fmk 20 billion (4 percent of GDP) for its operations, which included providing bank equity and granting loans and guarantees. In deciding on the appropriate support measures, the fund was guided by general principles, such as the transparency of support, relying on the bank owners' responsibility as much as possible, minimizing distortive effects, and ensuring public monitoring of supported banks.

---

[44]After the merger, 40 independent savings banks remained in business (Nyberg, 1994).

Table 15. Finland: Funds Used in Rescue Operations
(In millions of Finnish markkaa)

	Bank of Finland	Council of State				Government Guarantee Fund			Total
		State's capital investment	Preferred capital certificates	Share capital	Loan	Sub-ordinated loan	Preferred capital certificates	Share capital	
1991									
Skopbank	4,330								4,330
1992									
Skopbank	9,444	580				1,400	1,500	1,000	12,524
Savings Bank of Finland		1,094					7,100	2,900	12,494
Other savings banks		160							160
Security fund of the savings banks					500			500	
Okobank		422							422
Cooperative banks		1,108							1,108
Postipanki		903							903
Union Bank of Finland		1,749							1,749
KOP		1,726							1,726
STS-Bank		170							170
1993									
Skopbank	-2,722		350				1,200		-1,172
STS-Bank		-170					3,036		2,866
Savings Bank of Finland			750	250			950	150	2,100
Sale of Savings Bank of Finland		-1,094	-750				-3,756		-5,600
Asset management company Arsenal Ltd.				3,442				1,558	5,000
Security fund of the savings banks					-345				-345
Transfer to the Government Guarantee Fund					-357				-357
1994									
Asset-management company Arsenal Ltd.				6,000					6,000
1995									
Asset-management company Arsenal Ltd.				8,000					8,000
1996									
Asset-management company Arsenal Ltd.				4,000					4,000
Support disbursed as of December 1996	11,052	6,648	350	21,692	-202	1,400	10,030	5,608	56,578

Source: Finnish authorities.

company, majority-owned by the GGF. By October 1993, the Savings Bank of Finland had received a total of Fmk 14.6 billion (about 3 percent of GDP) from the Guarantee Fund.

Fearing a credit crunch as the equity position of banks threatened to fall below the Basle capital adequacy requirements in 1992, the government offered Fmk 7.9 billion as a capital injection to deposit banks proportional to their risk-weighted assets. The preferred capital certificates carried a noncumulative interest rate slightly above market rates and could thus be counted as Tier 1 capital.[45] If interest was not paid for three consecutive years or if a bank's equity ratio fell below the minimum required, the certificates could be converted into voting stock. All banks took advantage of the capital offer.

In October 1993, the business activities and the share capital of the Savings Bank of Finland were sold for Fmk 4 billion in equal parts to the four remaining banking groups, Kansallis Osake Pankki, Union Bank of Finland, Postbank, and the cooperative banks.[46] The nonperforming assets of the Savings Bank of Finland, valued at Fmk 40 billion, were transferred to a new asset-management company, Arsenal, whose losses were expected to reach Fmk 16 billion (see Nyberg and Vihriälä, 1994). Arsenal was funded with a Fmk 28 billion guarantee by the government. In mid-1994, however, Arsenal purchased a majority stake in the Savings Bank of Finland for Fmk 4 billion (equal to the original sales price) and took over the remaining assets from the GGF. By the end of 1996, Arsenal had received public bank support of Fmk 23 billion (in addition to government guarantees). The GGF had received in all Fmk 7.2 billion from the sale of the Savings Bank of Finland.

The third rescue operation involved Suomen Työväen Säästöpankki Bank (from herein referred to as STS Bank), which had been converted from a savings bank to a commercial bank in the late 1980s. Like many other savings banks, it suffered large credit losses from its rapid credit expansion, and its owners were unable to provide the necessary capital to keep the bank viable. Under close cooperation with the GGF, a merger of STS Bank with Kansallis Osake Pankki (forming the largest commercial bank in Finland) was negotiated in November 1992, in which the GGF would have assumed financial responsibility for most of the problem loans by transferring them to an asset-management company. Par-

liament, however, did not approve the formation of an asset-management company, and the merger had to be postponed.

In April 1993, a new merger agreement with Kansallis Osake Pankki was concluded. STS Bank itself was in effect turned into an asset-management company and retained all nonperforming loans and bad assets, while the rest of its banking business was transferred to Kansallis Osake Pankki. Although Kansallis Osake Pankki remained responsible for 10 percent of the losses on the portfolio of bad assets and had formal ownership of STS Bank, effective control rested with the GGF. As a result, the GGF anticipated a loss of Fmk 2.5 billion on STS Bank's Fmk 3.4 billion of nonperforming assets.

By the end of 1996, the total amount of public bank support disbursed was Fmk 56.6 billion (about 10 percent of GDP), with Fmk 35 billion for savings banks including Skopbank (Table 15). In addition, public guarantees of Fmk 32 billion had been granted, bringing the total amount of bank support to Fmk 88.6 billion (equivalent to 15.6 percent of GDP).

Banking Sector Performance Following the Banking Crises

Restructuring efforts in the aftermath of the banking crisis have led to significant changes in the structure of the banking sectors in all three countries. About four years after taking full ownership of the three largest banks, the Norwegian government completely privatized Fokus Bank in 1995 and has reduced its holdings in the two largest commercial banks to 72 percent and 51 percent, respectively. However, the public sector still has a significant stake in the financial system; the state holds a majority stake in financial institutions that account for more than 70 percent of commercial bank lending and half of total lending. With the exception of the state banks and the Postbank, state ownership in the banking system has its origins in the bank rescue operations.

In Sweden, two large-scale merger operations took place in the cooperative and savings bank groups, resulting in the creation of two large banks (Sparbanken Sverige and Föreningsbanken), which are listed on the Stockholm Stock Exchange. In particular, all cooperative banks were merged into one commercial bank. The consolidation process also intensified in Finland. At end-1996, the three largest banks accounted for about 80 percent of total assets of the deposit banks. The assets of the largest bank, Merita Bank—which was formed through the merger of the two major commercial banks (Kop and Unitas) in

---

[45]The interest rate on the certificates increases gradually relative to the market rate to give banks an incentive to repay bank support early.

[46]As part of the sale of the SBF, the government received share capital of Fmk 1 billion from Kansallis Osake Pankki and Fmk 0.5 billion from Union Bank of Finland.

Table 16. Bank Profitability: International Comparisons, 1990–94
(In percent of balance-sheet total; average)

	Net Interest Income (Intermediation margin)	Net Noninterest Income	Net Banking Income (Overall gross margin)	Total Operating Expenses	Pre-Tax Profit
Belgium	1.39	0.43	1.82	1.26	0.30
Denmark	3.44	0.17	3.60	2.38	−0.19
Finland	**1.61**	**1.78**	**3.39**	**3.00**	**−1.14**
France	1.59	0.70	2.30	1.52	0.24
Germany	1.96	0.60	2.57	1.63	0.52
Italy	3.22	1.15	4.37	2.66	1.09
Netherlands	1.73	0.70	2.44	1.65	0.50
Norway	**3.48**	**0.93**	**4.40**	**2.88**	**−0.33**
Portugal	3.69	1.10	4.79	2.35	1.07
Spain	3.39	0.89	4.28	2.56	0.93
Sweden	**2.69**	**1.79**	**4.48**	**2.42**	**1.12**
Switzerland	1.54	1.58	3.12	1.65	0.58
United Kingdom	2.57	1.85	4.42	2.87	0.64
Mean	**2.48**	**1.05**	**3.54**	**2.28**	**0.41**

Source: Malkamäki and Vesala (1996).
Note: Figures are average ratios 1990–94.

mid-1995—represent about 50 percent of total bank assets.

Loan losses have decreased in all three Nordic countries since 1994, primarily because of the recovery of their economies (see Koskenkylä, 1994). The economic recession was most severe in Finland and Sweden, while in Norway real GDP growth was stable during the 1990s. Bank lending has not yet fully recovered from its decline in the early 1990s, particularly in Finland, as companies have continued to finance their investments mainly with retained earnings and new share capital, in an effort to further reduce their indebtedness. While the banking systems in Norway and Sweden had returned to profitability by 1993 and 1994, respectively, Finnish banks only regained profitability in 1996 (Table 7 and Malkamäki and Vesala, 1996).[47]

Since 1993, the capital adequacy of the banks in all three countries has improved significantly with the help of considerable state support. In 1996, the average capital adequacy ratios were 12.4, 14, and 16 percent for Finland, Norway, and Sweden, respectively.[48]

Among the three Nordic countries, Finnish banks had the lowest ratio of net interest income to total assets, reflecting the existence of a large amount of nonperforming loans and the lack of demand for loans (Table 16). In 1994, Finland recorded the largest amounts of nonperforming loans among the Nordic countries. The weak demand for bank loans has increased bank competition, which was also reflected in declining interest rate margins. Interest rate margins in Finland are expected to be subject to further downward pressure, which will reduce banks' profitability and require further streamlining of their operations. In contrast to Finland, in Norway and Sweden the ratio of net interest income to total assets has increased since the banking crisis (Tables 8, 9, and 10).

The ratio of banks' operating expenses to total assets has decreased most sharply in Finland although most of this decline took place prior to the banking crisis (Tables 8, 9, and 10). The declining trend in Finland bottomed out, notwithstanding the severity of the Finnish banking crisis. Although the numbers of staff and bank branches have been reduced considerably (Table 2), with the exception of Norway,[49]

[47]Banks' profitability was further weakened in 1995 owing to losses in securities transactions, which were not connected to the banking crisis.
[48]Bank for International Settlements (1996).

[49]During 1987–94, the number of staff years employed in the commercial and savings bank sectors declined by 35 percent and 9 percent, respectively.

these developments have not yet been reflected in the trend of expenses in Finland and Sweden. This may partly be due to higher restructuring costs, including more generous severance packages, compared with Norway.

Although the banks' situation has improved in the aftermath of the banking crises, competition in the banking sector has increased, and the demand for loans is projected to continue to be sluggish. With increased financial integration in Europe, foreign banks are likely to increase their supply of services in the Nordic countries, increasing competition and further heightening the need for the Nordic banks to improve their efficiency. The need to reduce costs, in particular for bank staff, is especially strong in Finland, where the banks have more employees than other Nordic banks.

Lessons from the Bank Restructuring Operations

The three Nordic countries have taken different approaches to bank restructuring, as described above. Although it is difficult to make a robust evaluation of the outcome of these operations, several factors seem to suggest that Sweden's approach has been the most successful. In Finland, the banking system returned to profitability only in 1996, and in Norway the government still remains the major shareholder of the banking system. The decision to adopt a comprehensive strategy enabled Sweden to weather a severe crisis, maintain the country's credit rating, and minimize the costs of the restructuring program. The main principles underlying the success of Sweden's bank restructuring strategy can be summarized as follows:[50]

The key element of the restructuring program was the formation of a broad political consensus. This consensus was supported by timely information to all domestic parties. Transparency and disclosure of information were crucial for regaining confidence domestically and abroad; the implications of support measures for depositors and investors were extensively reported.

It was decided that to place the lead restructuring agency within existing institutions, such as the Ministry of Finance or the Riksbank, might have interfered adversely with the roles of these institutions.

Therefore, a separate institution—the Bank Support Authority—was created to implement the bank restructuring strategy. The formation of an institutional framework clarified the respective roles for the Ministry of Finance, the Riksbank, the Financial Supervisory Authority, and the Bank Support Authority. At the same time, there was a continuous exchange of information among the institutions.

Diagnosis was the first step in the restructuring exercise. A common yardstick—based on the capital adequacy ratio and other financial ratios—was designed to measure the degree of problems in banks. Initially, the banks were divided into two main categories: those that were considered viable and those that were not. While banks in the first category received support, the ones in the second category were closed or merged, and the banks' creditors were paid off.

Distorted incentives were minimized through the conditionality measures embedded in support agreements. The foremost conditions included changing management and upgrades of internal control and risk-management systems (which in most cases were found to be inadequate). The parliamentary guarantee did not cover owners' equity capital; in case of financial support by the government, owners typically lost their equity stakes.

Structural reforms of the accounting, legal, and regulatory framework and of prudential supervision were enacted. Clear guidelines on asset classification and valuation of banks' holdings of collateral (real estate and other assets) were set, with the Bank Support Authority monitoring compliance with these procedures.

The establishment of institutions for loan workout was given high priority. Problem assets were transferred, at an assumed market price,[51] to a separate asset-management company. As with other types of support provided to the banks, strict conditionality was attached to these operations. This approach facilitated the orderly sale of assets and allowed problem banks to continue their usual business without having to handle a large volume of workout cases. The asset-management company could recruit the specific expertise needed for transforming the bad assets into salable assets. The Bank Support Authority funded the asset-management companies and was their sole owner.

---

[50]These principles are outlined in Ingves and Lind (1996).

[51]The key concern was to make sure that all potential losses were borne by banks rather than the asset-management companies.

VII   Conclusions

Financial deregulation expands lenders' and borrowers' opportunities and capabilities for taking risks. As the Nordic experiences illustrate, if inappropriate incentives coincide with a macroeconomic environment that provides expansionary impulses at the time of deregulation, borrowers and lenders tend to behave in an unsustainable fashion. As a result, the domestic economy can overheat, fueled by rapidly rising asset prices.

Against the background of a quite stable and predictable—yet highly regulated—financial system, the deregulation efforts of the Nordic countries in the mid-1980s were a significant shock to the system. The elimination of direct controls on lending and exchange restrictions triggered a stock-adjustment effect in the debt burden of borrowers whose access to credit had previously been rationed and a surge in lending by banks that gained access to new funding sources. Although these initial stock-adjustment effects were inevitable, certain conditions and policy decisions that prevailed in the three Nordic countries played a critical role in magnifying these initial effects.

For the borrowers, the surge in asset prices during the boom years allowed households and firms to sharply increase their indebtedness without a significant effect on their net wealth. Important factors behind the aggressive borrowing included (1) expectations of rapid economic growth and asset price increases as the deregulation coincided with a strong macroeconomic momentum; (2) the low, and sometimes even negative, costs of borrowing (especially for real estate) owing to tax incentives and a policy of low interest rates combined with persistent high inflationary expectations; and (3) a highly leveraged corporate sector.

The resulting breakdown of traditional banking relationships that followed liberalization weakened banks' ability to assess credit risks and monitor borrowers and made it easier for financial institutions to enter new segments of the credit market. This, in turn, heightened competitive pressures further. In addition, the banking systems were characterized by relatively high operating costs and low profitability by international standards.[52] The high operating costs, which resulted primarily from large banking capacity, reinforced the managerial incentives for aggressive lending growth when the vast branch networks threatened to become unsustainable after deregulation. The aggressive bank lending policies were accompanied by a noticeable increase in risk taking. The composition of loan portfolios was shifted toward more cyclical sectors, and loans denominated in foreign currency rose sharply. In all three countries, loans appear to have been underpriced because of competition, and no additional operating profits were being generated to compensate for the greater lending risks, thus increasing the vulnerability of banks to credit losses. Important factors behind the aggressive lending by banks include (1) banks' relatively thin capitalization; (2) the reduced scope for managerial discretion; (3) the slow response of banks to adapt their internal risk-management and credit policies (including complicated cross shareholdings with nonfinancial corporations); and (4) the underestimation of the risks involved in asset-based lending.

It is also evident that policymakers did not take adequate measures to minimize the adjustment costs in the aftermath of the financial deregulation. The authorities failed to tighten prudential bank regulation and to create an adequate supervisory framework to take into account the substantial increase in banks' exposure to real estate lending and lending in foreign currency. The favorable tax treatment of interest payments was not reformed until well after the credit boom. Monetary policy was constrained by the fixed-exchange-rate regime, and the stance of fiscal policy was not tightened in a timely manner and to a sufficient extent.

The Nordic experience confirms that the incentives that accompany deregulation are crucial in transmitting the positive aspects of financial liberalization. In

---

[52]With the exception of Scandinaviska Enskilda Banken in Sweden, which was rated one of the most profitable banks in the world.

that connection, it is imperative that banks have a generous equity position and that banking overcapacity that may have built up under the previous regulatory regime is reduced prior to deregulation.

Close attention needs to be paid to the macroeconomic context of financial liberalization. In particular, monetary conditions have to be monitored carefully following liberalization to prevent the initial jump in asset prices from developing into a speculative bubble. In light of these macroeconomic uncertainties, it is essential that, parallel to deregulation, banks strengthen their internal management controls and especially their risk management. These efforts should, in addition, be supported and enforced by an adequate supervisory framework.

If banks do not take these steps and if the liberalization process is not designed carefully, problems will emerge. The competitive pressures that are typically enhanced by liberalization and the distortions in the incentive scheme caused by policy measures and the inherent structure of the financial sector will magnify the impact of a negative shock to the system and will threaten the stability of the entire financial system.

References

Abrams, Richard K., 1988, "The Financial Reform in Finland," IMF Working Paper 88/89 (Washington: International Monetary Fund).

Aranko, Jorma, 1994, "Reorganization of Financial Market Supervision in Finland," *Bank of Finland Bulletin,* Special Issue (Finland), pp. 36–40.

Bank for International Settlements, 1996, *Annual Report* (Basle, Switzerland).

Bank Support Authority, 1993, *Annual Review July 1, 1993–June 30, 1994,* Sweden.

Berg, Sigbjorn Atle, Finn R. Forsund, and Eilev S. Jansen, 1992, "Malmquist Indices of Productivity Growth During the Deregulation of Norwegian Banking, 1980–89," *Scandinavian Journal of Economics,* Vol. 94 (Supplement), pp. S211–28.

Berg, Sigbjorn Atle, and others, 1993, "Banking Efficiency in the Nordic Countries," *Journal of Banking and Finance,* Vol. 17 (April), pp. 371–88.

Biljer, Marianne, 1991, "Finance Companies: Structural Changes," *Quarterly Review,* Sveriges Riksbank, No. 3, pp. 5–13.

Bisat, Amer, R. Barry Johnston, and V. Sundararajan, 1992, "Issues in Managing and Sequencing Financial Sector Reforms: Lessons from Experiences in Five Developing Countries," IMF Working Paper 92/82 (Washington: International Monetary Fund).

Brunila, Anne, and Kari Takala, 1993, "Private Indebtedness and the Banking Crisis in Finland," Bank of Finland Discussion Paper 9/93 (Helsinki: Bank of Finland).

Calvo, Guillermo A., 1988, "Servicing the Public Dept: The Role of Expectations," *American Economic Review,* Vol. 78 (September), pp. 647–61.

Commission on the Banking Crisis, 1992, *Norwegian Official Reports* No. 30E, Oslo Government Printing Service (Norway).

Cottarelli, Carlo, and Angeliki Kourelis, 1994, "Financial Structure, Bank Lending Rates, and the Transmission Mechanism of Monetary Policy," *Staff Papers,* International Monetary Fund, Vol. 41 (December), pp. 587–623.

Cottarelli, Carlo, Giovanni Ferri, and Andrea Generale, 1995, "Bank Lending Rates and Financial Structure in Italy," *Staff Papers,* International Monetary Fund, Vol. 42 (September), pp. 670–700.

Dahleim, Bo, Goran Lind, and Anna-Karin Nedersjo, 1993, "The Banking Sector in 1992," *Quarterly Review,* Sveriges Riksbank (Sweden), Vol. 2 (June) pp. 24–36.

Davis, E. Philip, 1995, "Financial Fragility in the Early 1990s: What Can Be Learned from International Experience?" *Special Paper Series* (London: London School of Economics and Political Science).

Englund, Peter, 1990, "Financial Deregulation in Sweden," *European Economic Review,* Vol. 34 (May), pp. 385–93.

Fries, Steven M., 1993, "Japanese Banks and the Asset 'Price Bubble'," IMF Working Paper 93/85 (Washington: International Monetary Fund).

Furlong, Frederick T., and Michael C. Keeley, 1989, "Capital Regulation and Risk Taking: A Note," *Journal of Banking and Finance,* Vol. 13 (December), pp. 883–91.

Goldstein, Morris, and others, 1993, *International Capital Markets, Part II: Systemic Issues in International Finance,* World Economic and Financial Surveys (Washington: International Monetary Fund).

Gottfries, Nils, Christian B. Nilsson, and Kerstin Ohlsson, 1992, "Has Swedish Monetary Policy Been Countercyclical?" Sveriges Riksbank Working Paper No.7 (Sweden: Sveriges Riksbank, June).

Gottfries, Nils, Torsten Persson, and Edward Palmer, 1989, "Regulation, Financial Buffer Stocks, and Short-Run Adjustment: An Econometric Case Study of Sweden, 1970–82," *European Economic Review,* Vol. 33 (July), pp. 1546–565.

Guttentag, Jack M., and Richard J. Herring, 1986, "Disaster Myopia in International Banking," Essays in International Finance No. 164 (Princeton, New Jersey: Princeton University).

Hubbard, Glenn, ed., 1991, "Financial Markets and Financial Crises" (Chicago: University of Chicago Press).

Ingves, Stefan, and Göran Lind, 1996, "The Management of the Bank Crisis in Retrospect," *Quarterly Review,* Sveriges Riksbank (Sweden), No. 1, pp. 5–18.

International Monetary Fund, 1996, "Norway—Background Paper," IMF Staff Country Report, No. 96/15 (Washington).

Jonung, Lars, 1986, "Financial Deregulation in Sweden," *Quarterly Review,* Skandinaviska Enskilda Banken, Vol. 4 (December), pp. 109–19.

——, Hans Tson Soderstrom, and Joakim Stymne, 1994, "Depression in the North: Boom and Bust in Sweden and Finland, 1985–93," IMF Seminar Series, No. 1994-47 (Washington: International Monetary Fund).

Keeley, Michael C., 1990, "Deposit Insurance, Risk, and Market Power in Banking," *American Economic Review,* Vol. 80 (December), pp. 1183–200.

Koskenkylä, Heikki, 1994, "The Nordic Banking Crisis," *Bank of Finland Bulletin,* Vol. 68 (August), pp. 15–22.

——, and Jukka Vesala, 1994, "Finnish Deposit Banks 1980–1993: Years of Rapid Growth and Crisis," Bank of Finland Discussion Paper, No. 16/94 (Helsinki: Bank of Finland).

Lehmussaari, Olli-Pekka, 1990, "Deregulation and Consumption: Saving Dynamics in the Nordic Countries," *Staff Papers,* International Monetary Fund, Vol. 37 (March), pp. 71–93.

Llewellyn, David T., 1992, "The Performance of Banks in the U.K. and Scandinavia: A Case Study in Competition and Deregulation," *Quarterly Review,* Sveriges Riksbank (Sweden), Vol. 3 (September), pp. 20–30.

Lind, Göran, and Anna-Karin Nedersjo, 1994, "The Banking Sector in 1993," *Quarterly Review,* Sveriges Riksbank (Sweden), Vol. 2 (June), pp. 24–35.

Malkamäki, Markku, and Jukka Vesala, 1996, "Finnish Financial Markets: Major Trends and International Comparisons," *Bank of Finland Bulletin,* Special Issue (Helsinki: Bank of Finland), pp. 5–21.

Minsky, Hyman P., 1977, "A Theory of Systematic Fragility," in *Financial Crises: Institutions and Markets in a Fragile Environment,* ed. by Edward I. Altman and Arnold W. Sametz (New York).

Nyberg, Peter, 1994, "Decision on the Restructuring of the Savings Bank Sector," *Bank of Finland Bulletin,* Vol. 68, No. 1, pp. 5–7.

——, and Vesa Vihriälä, 1994, "Finnish Banking Crisis and Its Handling," Bank of Finland Discussion Paper, 7/94 (Helsinki: Bank of Finland).

Organization for Economic Cooperation and Development, 1995, *Economic Surveys: Norway* (Paris).

——, *Bank Profitability,* various issues (Paris).

Pazarbaşıoğlu, Ceyla, 1997, "A Credit Crunch? Finland in the Aftermath of the Banking Crisis," *Staff Papers,* International Monetary Fund, Vol. 44 (September), pp. 315–27.

Pensala, Johanna, and Heikki Solttila, 1993, "Banks' Nonperforming Assets and Write-Offs in 1992," Bank of Finland Discussion Paper 10/93 (Helsinki: Bank of Finland).

Persson, Torsten, and Guido Tabellini, 1990, *Macroeconomic Policy, Credibility, and Politics* (New York: Harwood Academic Publishers).

Schuijer, Jan, 1992, *Banks Under Stress* (Paris: Organization for Economic Cooperation and Development).

Shrieves, Ronald E., and Drew Dahl, 1992, "The Relationship Between Risk and Capital in Commercial Banks," *Journal of Banking and Finance,* Vol. 16 (April), pp. 439–57.

Solttila, Heikki, and Vesa Vihriälä, 1994, "Finnish Banks' Problem Assets: Result of Unfortunate Asset Structure or Too Rapid Growth?" Bank of Finland Discussion Paper 23/94 (Helsinki: Bank of Finland).

Stiglitz, Joseph E., 1993, *The Role of the State in Financial Markets* (Washington: World Bank).

Sundararajan, V., and Tomás Baliño, 1991, "Issues in Recent Banking Crises," in *Banking Crises: Cases and Issues,* ed. by V. Sundararajan and T. J. T. Baliño, (Washington: International Monetary Fund).

Sveriges Riksbank, 1992, *Quarterly Review* (Stockholm: Central Bank of Sweden).

White, Lawrence J., 1991, *The S&L Debacle* (New York: Oxford University Press).

Wilse, Hans Petter, 1995, "Management of the Banking Crisis and State Ownership of Commercial Banks," Norges Bank, Economic Bulletin, No. 2 (Norway).

Recent Occasional Papers of the International Monetary Fund

161. The Nordic Banking Crises: Pitfalls in Financial Liberalization? by Burkhard Dress and Ceyla Pazarbaşıoğlu. 1998.

160. Fiscal Reform in Low-Income Countries: Experience Under IMF-Supported Programs, by a Staff Team led by George T. Abed and comprising Liam Ebrill, Sanjeev Gupta, Benedict Clements, Ronald Mc-Morran, Anthony Pellechio, Jerald Schiff, and Marijn Verhoeven. 1998.

159. Hungary: Economic Policies for Sustainable Growth, Carlo Cottarelli, Thomas Krueger, Reza Moghadam, Perry Perone, Edgardo Ruggiero, and Rachel van Elkan. 1998.

158. Transparency in Goverment Operations, by George Kopits and Jon Craig. 1998

157. Central Bank Reforms in the Baltics, Russia, and the Other Countries of the Former Soviet Union, by a Staff Team led by Malcolm Knight and comprising Susana Almuiña, John Dalton, Inci Otker, Ceyla Pazarbaşıoğlu, Arne B. Petersen, Peter Quirk, Nicholas M. Roberts, Gabriel Sensenbrenner, and Jan Willem van der Vossen. 1997.

156. The ESAF at Ten Years: Economic Adjustment and Reform in Low-Income Countries, by the Staff of the International Monetary Fund. 1997.

155. Fiscal Policy Issues During the Transition in Russia, by Augusto Lopez-Claros and Sergei Alexashenko. 1998.

154. Credibility Without Rules? Monetary Frameworks in the Post–Bretton Woods Era, by Carlo Cottarelli and Curzio Giannini. 1997.

153. Pension Regimes and Saving, by G.A. Mackenzie, Philip Gerson, and Alfredo Cuevas. 1997.

152. Hong Kong, China: Growth, Structural Change, and Economic Stability During the Transition, by John Dodsworth and Dubravko Mihaljek. 1997.

151. Currency Board Arrangements: Issues and Experiences, by a staff team led by Tomás J.T. Baliño and Charles Enoch. 1997.

150. Kuwait: From Reconstruction to Accumulation for Future Generations, by Nigel Andrew Chalk, Mohamed A. El-Erian, Susan J. Fennell, Alexei P. Kireyev, and John F. Wison. 1997.

149. The Composition of Fiscal Adjustment and Growth: Lessons from Fiscal Reforms in Eight Economies, by G.A. Mackenzie, David W.H. Orsmond, and Philip R. Gerson. 1997.

148. Nigeria: Experience with Structural Adjustment, by Gary Moser, Scott Rogers, and Reinold van Til, with Robin Kibuka and Inutu Lukonga. 1997.

147. Aging Populations and Public Pension Schemes, by Sheetal K. Chand and Albert Jaeger. 1996.

146. Thailand: The Road to Sustained Growth, by Kalpana Kochhar, Louis Dicks-Mireaux, Balazs Horvath, Mauro Mecagni, Erik Offerdal, and Jianping Zhou. 1996.

145. Exchange Rate Movements and Their Impact on Trade and Investment in the APEC Region, by Takatoshi Ito, Peter Isard, Steven Symansky, and Tamim Bayoumi. 1996.

144. National Bank of Poland: The Road to Indirect Instruments, by Piero Ugolini. 1996.

143. Adjustment for Growth: The African Experience, by Michael T. Hadjimichael, Michael Nowak, Robert Sharer, and Amor Tahari. 1996.

142. Quasi-Fiscal Operations of Public Financial Institutions, by G.A. Mackenzie and Peter Stella. 1996.

141. Monetary and Exchange System Reforms in China: An Experiment in Gradualism, by Hassanali Mehran, Marc Quintyn, Tom Nordman, and Bernard Laurens. 1996.

140. Government Reform in New Zealand, by Graham C. Scott. 1996.

139. Reinvigorating Growth in Developing Countries: Lessons from Adjustment Policies in Eight Economies, by David Goldsbrough, Sharmini Coorey, Louis Dicks-Mireaux, Balazs Horvath, Kalpana Kochhar, Mauro Mecagni, Erik Offerdal, and Jianping Zhou. 1996.

138. Aftermath of the CFA Franc Devaluation, by Jean A.P. Clément, with Johannes Mueller, Stéphane Cossé, and Jean Le Dem. 1996.

137. The Lao People's Democratic Republic: Systemic Transformation and Adjustment, edited by Ichiro Otani and Chi Do Pham. 1996.

136. Jordan: Strategy for Adjustment and Growth, edited by Edouard Maciejewski and Ahsan Mansur. 1996.

135. Vietnam: Transition to a Market Economy, by John R. Dodsworth, Erich Spitäller, Michael Braulke, Keon Hyok Lee, Kenneth Miranda, Christian Mulder, Hisanobu Shishido, and Krishna Srinivasan. 1996.

134. India: Economic Reform and Growth, by Ajai Chopra, Charles Collyns, Richard Hemming, and Karen Parker with Woosik Chu and Oliver Fratzscher. 1995.

133. Policy Experiences and Issues in the Baltics, Russia, and Other Countries of the Former Soviet Union, edited by Daniel A. Citrin and Ashok K. Lahiri. 1995.

132. Financial Fragilities in Latin America: The 1980s and 1990s, by Liliana Rojas-Suárez and Steven R. Weisbrod. 1995.

131. Capital Account Convertibility: Review of Experience and Implications for IMF Policies, by staff teams headed by Peter J. Quirk and Owen Evans. 1995.

130. Challenges to the Swedish Welfare State, by Desmond Lachman, Adam Bennett, John H. Green, Robert Hagemann, and Ramana Ramaswamy. 1995.

129. IMF Conditionality: Experience Under Stand-By and Extended Arrangements. Part II: Background Papers. Susan Schadler, Editor, with Adam Bennett, Maria Carkovic, Louis Dicks-Mireaux, Mauro Mecagni, James H.J. Morsink, and Miguel A. Savastano. 1995.

128. IMF Conditionality: Experience Under Stand-By and Extended Arrangements. Part I: Key Issues and Findings, by Susan Schadler, Adam Bennett, Maria Carkovic, Louis Dicks-Mireaux, Mauro Mecagni, James H.J. Morsink, and Miguel A. Savastano. 1995.

127. Road Maps of the Transition: The Baltics, the Czech Republic, Hungary, and Russia, by Biswajit Banerjee, Vincent Koen, Thomas Krueger, Mark S. Lutz, Michael Marrese, and Tapio O. Saavalainen. 1995.

126. The Adoption of Indirect Instruments of Monetary Policy, by a staff team headed by William E. Alexander, Tomás J.T. Baliño, and Charles Enoch. 1995.

125. United Germany: The First Five Years—Performance and Policy Issues, by Robert Corker, Robert A. Feldman, Karl Habermeier, Hari Vittas, and Tessa van der Willigen. 1995.

124. Saving Behavior and the Asset Price "Bubble" in Japan: Analytical Studies, edited by Ulrich Baumgartner and Guy Meredith. 1995.

123. Comprehensive Tax Reform: The Colombian Experience, edited by Parthasarathi Shome. 1995.

122. Capital Flows in the APEC Region, edited by Mohsin S. Khan and Carmen M. Reinhart. 1995.

121. Uganda: Adjustment with Growth, 1987–94, by Robert L. Sharer, Hema R. De Zoysa, and Calvin A. McDonald. 1995.

120. Economic Dislocation and Recovery in Lebanon, by Sena Eken, Paul Cashin, S. Nuri Erbas, Jose Martelino, and Adnan Mazarei. 1995.

119. Singapore: A Case Study in Rapid Development, edited by Kenneth Bercuson with a staff team comprising Robert G. Carling, Aasim M. Husain, Thomas Rumbaugh, and Rachel van Elkan. 1995.

118. Sub-Saharan Africa: Growth, Savings, and Investment, by Michael T. Hadjimichael, Dhaneshwar Ghura, Martin Mühleisen, Roger Nord, and E. Murat Uçer. 1995.

117. Resilience and Growth Through Sustained Adjustment: The Moroccan Experience, by Saleh M. Nsouli, Sena Eken, Klaus Enders, Van-Can Thai, Jörg Decressin, and Filippo Cartiglia, with Janet Bungay. 1995.

116. Improving the International Monetary System: Constraints and Possibilities, by Michael Mussa, Morris Goldstein, Peter B. Clark, Donald J. Mathieson, and Tamim Bayoumi. 1994.

115. Exchange Rates and Economic Fundamentals: A Framework for Analysis, by Peter B. Clark, Leonardo Bartolini, Tamim Bayoumi, and Steven Symansky. 1994.

Note: For information on the title and availability of Occasional Papers not listed, please consult the IMF Publications Catalog or contact IMF Publication Services.